Freshman in the Kitchen
From Clueless Cook to Creative Chef

Freshman in

From Clueless Cook to Creative Chef   Max and Eli Sussman

the Kitchen

All inquiries should be addressed to:
Huron River Press
308½ South State Street, Suite 30
Ann Arbor, Michigan 48104
www.huronriverpress.com

Printed and bound in Thailand

10 9 8 7 6 5 4 3 2 1

Library of Congress Cataloging-in-Publication Data

Sussman, Eli, 1985-
  Freshman in the kitchen : from clueless cook to creative chef / by Eli and
Max Sussman.
     p. cm.
  Includes index.
  ISBN 1-932399-18-6
  1. Cookery. I. Sussman, Max, 1982- II. Title.
  TX651.S87 2008
  641.5--dc22

                              2008012163

Photographers:
Steve Klein
R. H. Hensleigh
Kate McCabe
Max Sussman

Design:
Savitski Design

Hey! Thanks for buying our cookbook!

We are Max and Eli Sussman. We are brothers from Michigan and we are avid cooks. Neither of us are fancy celebrity chefs with a TV show but we do got skills; bill payin' skills that is. Combined, we have years of experience in a broad range of cooking environments including restaurants, catering, private homes and at our childhood camp running the kitchen for several summers. We wrote this as a guide not just to help you learn how to cook, but to become passionate about food as well.

We realize that people our age sometimes get a bad rap for being lazy and uninterested in trying new things. We wrote this book to help you learn how to cook, starting with simple recipes and then getting increasingly more challenging as the chapters progress. Don't worry if you've never even made toast and don't turn away if you have cooked a three-course meal before. There's something in here for everyone, no matter how experienced or inexperienced you are.

Some of the most common excuses why not to cook are no time, money, or know-how. This cookbook helps with all those problems. It's like your own personal cooking teacher. We have included little tips throughout to give you creative ideas on how to be resourceful, inventive and have fun while cooking. Armed with this book, easy-to-find ingredients, and your effort; you can make yourself an entire meal for less than the cost of delivery. Have fun and impress your family, friends and even surprise yourself.

You know the saying, "There are no dumb questions." Well, we will roll with that because we don't want to hurt your feelings. We promise to answer any cooking question you ask. Questions like how do I make grilled cheese? What is sautéing? How do I boil pasta? How do I preheat an oven? What is deglazing? Unlike other cookbook authors, we won't assume that you have even one second of cooking experience. We want you to go ahead and mess up, substitute, learn

Now let's look at the keys that will help you navigate this book.

 = Type of dish (salad, etc.)

 = Number of Servings

 = Time to prepare the dish

 = Time Saving Tip

 = Money Saving Tip

 = Helpful Hints

from your mistakes, and make up your own food creations — after all, that's how we learned.

It's cooking made easy brought to you in a new way that you can relate to. It's *Freshman in the Kitchen*.

"Where'd you guys learn to cook like that?"

We remember two distinct types of kitchens from our childhood. There was our kitchen . . . and then there was everyone else's. We didn't have a microwave (and yes, we believed at the time that this was the greatest travesty in human history). We rarely had cookies and junk food like potato chips, and gummy candies never made the cut into our kitchen (or into our lunches). We were deprived of store-bought salad dressings and microwavable pizza bagels, chicken nuggets, complete meals in plastic trays and soda pop. Yes, our life was hard.

It seemed like our friends' cupboards were stocked with snacks floor to ceiling and the freezer was loaded with every microwavable meal invented. We reluctantly returned home after hanging out with friends to a fridge filled with fresh fruits, endless vegetables and an extensive drink selection consisting of orange juice or milk. Don't get us wrong — it's not that we had a problem with our friends' food choices (in fact, we loved going to their houses to eat junk food). But our house was different. It was just how it was and the fact that our mom cooked every meal from scratch was just how it was going to be.

As kids we couldn't understand — what were the evils of all these pre-made and microwavable foods? What did store-bought Ranch Dressing do to offend our parents so deeply? We found out that our parents made these food choices for two reasons. First, they figured it would be a healthier way to eat, and second, because they both love to cook. This trait got passed along to us.

Our love for cooking and food in general was born out of the unique choices our parents made in our home. Our mom's ability to innovate in the kitchen and cook from scratch has led to dozens of incredible meals that have become part of our own staple of dishes we love to cook. Her London Broil, stir-fries, and original salads with homemade dressings led us to develop a sophisticated palate and love for eating and creating food. Our dad's lamb stew, from-scratch sauces and famous homemade breads, often using Michigan fruit, let us know that taking time and doing it right can yield incredible cuisine. We saw the joy our parents got from cooking and the impressions it left on guests and family who were consistently surprised and impressed when they came over to eat.

As we got older we moved from licking the spoon after our mom made brownies (not from a package!) to assisting with cooking for big family dinners. Seeing both pre-made and from-scratch food, we now have come to seriously appreciate all the cooking our parents did for us (even if it did require waiting a bit longer to eat!). We know that our passion, creativity and drive to be the best cooks possible came from our parents. And yes, to this day, our parents do not have a microwave.

Stocking up your Kitchen

Essential
Kitchen tongs: A good set of tongs might be the most surprisingly good purchase you make. With tongs, you can move hot things around in a pan with more dexterity than a spatula, stir hot liquids, and reach into a hot oven to grab something.
Set of dry measuring cups: For baking and measuring dry goods.
Large strainer/colander: A must for draining pasta, and very helpful for washing vegetables.
Cutting board: Unless you have a custom kitchen you designed yourself, you probably have plastic-type counters. If you try to cut directly on them, you will scratch them and then your landlord will

not be happy. Get a few cutting boards so that friends can help prep if they want. A cutting board is portable, so you can easily move those diced onions over to your sauté pan and dump them right in (carefully, of course).

Glass 2-cup measuring cup: Measure liquids in a glass measuring cup, since you can look at the side to know when you have the right amount, and then you won't spill all over the place.

Set of measuring spoons: Another must-have for baking. Don't ever try to eyeball 1/4 teaspoon of baking soda or disaster will undoubtedly ensue.

Large mixing spoon (wood): A wooden spoon is great for stirring soup or anything else hot. Since it doesn't conduct heat it won't burn your hand. It is also great for sautéing in nonstick pans.

Large plastic spatula: Really nothing else will work to flip a pancake than a nice large plastic spatula, and it won't scratch your nonstick pan either.

Silicone Spatula: This looks like a rubber spatula, but is made of heat-resistant silicone and is important if you don't want melted plastic in your eggs.

Box grater: It's less expensive to buy blocks of cheese and grate it yourself, and it also tastes better. The various edges on a box grater can be used to grate carrots, ginger, onions, and garlic.

Vegetable peeler: Without it, how could you peel vegetables?

Food Processor or Blender: One of the most versatile pieces of equipment you can buy, a food processor can do nearly everything a blender can do and more, so we recommend it.

Whisk: This is a three-dimensional wire tool that is used for whipping ingredients, thereby incorporating air into them. Very handy.

Cutlery

Chef Knife: This knife is incredibly versatile. It can be used for everything from dicing onions to slicing cheese to carving a chicken. You can find a decent knife for under $50, but if you cook often, you might want to invest in a more expensive knife. A good knife should rest more comfortably in your hand, so go to a store that has a wide selection and ask to see some of them.

A Note on Knives

Knives are one of a cook's best friends. Treat them well and they will do the same for you. Keep your knives in good shape by cleaning them right after you use them (certain foods will dry quickly on the knife and can be hard to clean later). Keep your knives sharp by having them sharpened professionally or doing it yourself. Either way, you should keep a sharpening steel in your kitchen to hone (as opposed to sharpen) the blade on your knives regularly. A sharp knife will not only be much better to work with (especially when trying to finely cut delicate foods) but will be safer too, as it will go where you point it as opposed to sliding off and going in a different direction.

Paring Knife: Useful for peeling fruit and cutting more delicate and small items.

Serrated Bread Knife: Besides slicing bread, this knife has a range of uses, including very soft tomatoes (if your chef knife isn't razor sharp).

Pots and Pans

Large (6 to 8-quart) heavy-bottomed stockpot with lid: From sautéing onions and garlic to keeping an even heat during simmering, this is the only thing that will consistently make great soup. The heavy bottom will keep your onions from burning, and the ample size will be more than enough for boiling pasta. We recommend a non-aluminum pot since metal can impart an off flavor to acidic foods.

2-quart heavy-bottomed saucepan: Great for making sauce or reducing liquid. Again, the heavy bottom is a must.

Two 8 or 10-inch nonstick skillets: We've heard that they made omelets and crepes before they had nonstick pans, but we don't believe it.

One 10-inch sauté/frying pan: Whatever you call it, this is one of the most important pans to have. If you already have a nonstick skillet, the next addition to your pan department should be a regular old stainless steel frying pan. For pan-searing meat and all sautéing needs, this frying pan is key.

1 large casserole dish (9 x 13) with raised edges: For Mac and Cheese, and other similar baked dishes, this is an absolute must-have.

1–2 sheet pans: While all types of baking pans can be found, we recommend the old standard sheet pan, "half-sheet" size. Get 2 and you can have cookies in almost no time.

Splurge

Small pastry or BBQ brush: From brushing on marinade to other baking uses, this inexpensive tool is nice to have around.

Fine and/or Medium Microplane: Microplane makes a specialized grating tool that is very helpful for zesting lemons or oranges, and the medium grater can be used to grate chocolate, ginger, garlic or other unwieldy ingredients.

8-cup heatproof glass measuring cup: This one might seem out of the blue, but it has come in handy so many times that it easily made it onto this list. If while making soup, you realize you need your only large pot for simmering something else, you will be very happy to have this glass dish in your cupboard.

Offset Spatula: This spatula has an offset blade so that you can spread icing without your hand getting in the way.

Wire Cooling Rack: If you bake a lot of cookies, a wire cooling rack is a helpful addition to any kitchen.

Grocery Shopping

We know that everyone has at least one activity they dread. For a lot of people it's the clichéd visit to the dentist. Others may be highly opposed to doing laundry, dishes or cleaning their room (for most of the people we have lived with it's all three. Burn!).

The visit to the grocery store can cause great anxiety. Cruising the aisles with a rickety cart, wheels squeaking on the brightly lit linoleum floor of a warehouse-sized open room, with hundreds of strangers around, all while your ears are assaulted with the lush tones of a Kenny G knockoff can make any person queasy. To get in and out with as little hassle and as much efficiency as possible, we've created some golden rules to use when grocery shopping.

Always Eat Before You Go (You will buy less things you don't even want.)

Going hungry to the supermarket is like letting Harold and Kumar loose in a White Castle with a platinum credit card. When faced with the dilemma of two things that you want to purchase, logic will cease to exist and you will choose both. This can be devastating when you come in to the parking lot with an empty wallet and 3 boxes of frozen bagel-egg-sausage sandwiches that will NOT taste as good as they look on the box.

Make a List — Check it once. (Checking it twice gets us in copyright trouble.)

Making a list will help you decide beforehand what you really want and can afford. Following our list of rules is a breakdown of what can be purchased within certain grocery shopping budgets. It contains a lot of what we have deemed "essential items" that can be used in several dishes. The less useless items you buy the more $'s you will have for stuff you really need.

Less is More (Actually less is less, this is undeniable.)

Be very careful for promotions that encourage you to buy several items for a reduced price. If you need to buy ten of something to save a dollar, is it really worth having ten of that item? Will it go bad? Unless you are having a frosting fight don't buy 6 tubs of it. Also, a lot of those deals are because they can't get rid of all the stock. If no one else is buying it, then you probably shouldn't buy five no matter how cheap it may be. Also, you can often buy just one of the "two for one deal" and get a cheaper price. I know you hate math, but a little addition and subtraction never killed anyone.

Hey You Guys! Wear Something That Has Pockets (Or just carry a "murse", which is a man purse.)

Women are smart. They have a purse and it holds everything just short of another car in case their original vehicle dies. Guys on the other hand are unprepared. Just from experience shopping in basketball shorts and other pocketless garb, you end up having

nowhere to put your keys, cell phone, wallet and the list that you should have made if you followed rule #2. Without pockets you end up putting it all in the cart, but the keys and cell phone always fall through some slot or hole so you end up having to hold them in your hand while wheeling the cart...anyways it is a devastating experience...let's move on.

Don't Check Out the Self-Checkout

Self-checkout is dumb. Period. It never works properly and you often end up having to call over the real person to help you figure out all the computer prompts, which really defeats the entire purpose of doing self-checkout. Also, if you embrace self-checkout, soon computers will phase out all workers and you will lose your job. We know, that is a pretty intense scenario, but don't complain to us when the robot screws up your order at Subway. We totally warned you.

Getting to Know Your Ingredients

We realize that for certain items, they are much more convenient to purchase already made than to spend your valuable time making them from scratch. You are already too busy checking your e-mail to squeeze in sleeping, so we don't actually believe you are going to make your own mustard or ketchup. We do suggest that you take a look at the ingredients on items before you buy them. As a general rule of thumb, the shorter the list of ingredients, the less likely it is to contain additives like high fructose corn syrup, fake colors and weird chemical preservatives. We aren't telling you to completely change everything you buy, just to take a look at ingredients and be aware of what you are putting in your body. If most of the ingredients sound like something out of *Star Trek* and have more numbers than letters, maybe check out a different version of the item.

The Best Chefs Know How To Shop

The odds are when you go to the supermarket you try to look for the best deals and cheapest items. While we understand this mentality (being pretty much broke ourselves), if you're cooking, it sometimes makes sense to spend a few extra dollars to get a better product. The reason is that if you have better ingredients, you're going to cook a better dish or meal. No amount of culinary know-how or experience can turn a pale, out-of-season, tasteless tomato that's flown halfway around the world into a bright red, juicy, and outrageously flavorful tomato that was picked yesterday in the farm less than an hour's drive away. Chefs in the best restaurants around the world know this and that's why they spend countless hours and dollars trying to get the best ingredients. If you're making a dish that features a certain ingredient prominently, or if you just want the best flavor possible, go out of your way to pick the best ingredients and you will be rewarded. You might even want to stop at a few stores, if one has a better butcher and one has fresher produce, for example.

Essentials and Staples
The items on the list below will keep for a decent amount of time. The dry goods will last for a year and the produce and refrigerated stuff should last a good week. These items are basically essential to have around the kitchen. When you are hungry and go to look for something to eat in your cupboard and find those potatoes or black beans you will be glad you have them. For other produce or if you're buying meat fresh (not frozen) you should get that stuff as you need it. Remember to buy wisely.

Herbs, Spices, and other powdered things:
Kosher Salt
Iodized Salt
Black Pepper
Garlic Powder
Crushed Red Pepper Flakes
Oregano
Basil
Cumin
Paprika
Thyme
Dill
Cayenne Pepper
Chili Powder

Condiments:
Ketchup
Mustard
Mayonnaise
BBQ Sauce
Soy Sauce
Chili Sauce

Dry Goods:
All-purpose Flour
Peanut Butter
Jelly
Spaghetti
Breadcrumbs
Penne Pasta
Angel Hair Pasta
Elbow Macaroni
White Rice
Brown Rice

Oils and Liquids:
Vegetable Oil
Extra Virgin Olive oil
Toasted Sesame Oil
Balsamic Vinegar
White Vinegar
Rice Vinegar

Canned Goods:
Black Beans
Pinto Beans
Garbanzo Beans
Whole Peeled Tomatoes
Tomato Paste
Tuna
Black/Green Olives
Corn

Perishable Goods/Produce
Butter
Milk
Potatoes
Onions
Garlic
Frozen Peas
Cheese
Cucumber
Tomato
Lettuce
Carrots
Bread
Broccoli

A note on bread

We love bread and use it in so many ways in many of our recipes. You can find bread for 50 cents but if there is one thing we would splurge on, it's good bread so you can make great sandwiches, French toast, croutons and stuffing. Any loaf of bread that can be compacted into a small ball in your hand or can sit out on the counter for weeks without going bad is not bread. It is weird chemicals in the shape of bread. Don't be fooled. Find a bakery near you and try it out; you won't be disappointed.

Max Helps You Buy Organic and Local

If you are reading this book, then you know there's something to be said for making food for yourself and others from scratch. There's really nothing comparable to the satisfaction that comes from a successful dish that you cooked and shared with friends or family. That feeling comes from having made everything yourself instead of buying it pre-packaged in a store.

You can get that same great feeling from buying food responsibly and thinking about your impact on the world we live in. Shortening the path between producer and consumer will provide you with food that tastes better. Look at the label on your vegetables — asparagus in winter in Michigan? They were picked a week ago and then flown in from hundreds or thousands of miles away, usually covered in chemicals.

Most produce bought in the supermarket is conventional, meaning it is sprayed with pesticides to keep bugs from eating it and to preserve it during transport. Buying organic produce means that you are putting less or no harmful chemicals in your body.

Lots of times organic and local are not the same thing. I try to support local farmers as much as possible. It's reassuring to be able to see and talk to the person that you know grew and harvested the food you're eating. Supporting local farmers is good for the

For more resources, you can visit these websites:

Local Harvest
http://localharvest.org

Eat Well
http://eatwellguide.com

Sustainable Table
http://sustainabletable.org

Freshman in the Kitchen
http://freshmaninthekitchen.com

community and the local economy. The food will be fresher and taste better as well.

Don't get me wrong, I buy fruit in the winter and it's definitely not from Michigan! And I drink coffee every day (fair trade of course). Not every item can be bought locally, but I do think it's important to be aware of these issues and to try to make a positive impact however I can.

Look around in your area for farmers markets or produce markets that stock local produce. In many areas you can become a member of a CSA (Community Supported Agriculture) and receive a fresh box of vegetables every week. Not only are you directly supporting the small farmers that work so hard to grow these fruits and vegetables, you also are getting the freshest and tastiest produce around.

getting

We both believe that food doesn't need to be complicated or fancy in order to be delicious. We both realize you are often on the run or need to throw something together that you can eat later where you won't have access to a kitchen, oven, or microwave.

In this chapter we have recipes that need little or no actual cooking (meaning heat) to prepare. The cooking time is also very short, under 15 minutes for many recipes. You should be able to follow these recipes even as a beginner cook.

From snacks to sandwiches to salads, this chapter gives you some great ideas for quick and easy dishes.

But don't think these recipes are any less tasty just because they're quick — you'll come back to them again and again for appetizers to start off a meal or salads to accompany your smashing entrée. And your friends will be begging you to make them appetizers and snacks every day.

Nice and Easy
Started

Bruschetta is a simple dish that always surprises with the rustic intensity of flavor. Use the ripest, best tomatoes you can find, and serve as soon as possible.

Bruschetta

Getting Started

Appetizer

Serves 4

Total Time 20 minutes

5 small diced ripe Roma or vine-ripened
   tomatoes, ½-inch pieces

3 fresh **garlic** cloves; 2 sliced, 1 reserved for
   rubbing baguette slices

⅓ cup fresh **basil**, chopped or chiffonade
   (see Cutting Herbs, page 127)

salt and **pepper**, to taste

2 tablespoons extra virgin **olive oil**

1 **baguette**

1 Dice tomatoes and place in mixing bowl. Add garlic, chopped basil, salt and pepper. Mix together. Add extra virgin olive oil and mix.

2 Slice baguette on angle into 1-inch slices. Rub both sides with cut garlic clove dipped in oil. Place on baking sheet and broil until golden (about 1 minute), flip and broil reverse side for about 1 minute.

3 Remove from oven. Place topping on slices using slotted spoon or regular spoon, being careful to drain juice. Find your nicest platter and serve them up.

Prosciutto Wrapped Green Olives

Getting Started

 Appetizer

 Serves 4–6

 Total time 10 minutes

1 can (12 ounce) large **green olives**
approximately 50 **toothpicks**
½ pound of thinly sliced **prosciutto**

This dish is classy and has a complex flavor. The younger set may not go crazy over this at the party or tailgate event but the older adults will be popping 'em like candy.

1 Drain the liquid from the olives.

2 Slice the prosciutto the short way into about 3-inch by ½-inch strips.

3 Take one olive and roll it up in the strip of prosciutto. Place a toothpick in each to hold it together. Repeat for all olives.

4 Arrange on a serving plate. Serve immediately or refrigerate.

Dicing, Chopping, and Mincing

Many recipes call for a dice, chop, or mince — these are just names for different ways of cutting.

A **dice** generally means cutting something into uniform cube shapes that can be up to 1/8-inch small (although none of our recipes call for anything that small). The best way to dice a vegetable is to first cut it into long strips, then stack or line up these strips and cut several at once. That way, your pieces are all the same size and they will cook at the same rate.

Chopping, on the other hand, means that pieces don't need to be a uniform shape. Finely chopped (fresh herbs, for example) means cutting something until you can't cut it any smaller. When it matters to how a dish turns out, our recipes have specific sizes listed as well. For more info on cutting herbs, see page 127.

Mincing is similar to finely chopping, but we use this word to refer to firmer objects (like garlic and ginger) whose flavor increases the smaller they get. Feel free to experiment using a medium flat-grater to make short work out of mincing ginger.

Asian Chicken Salad

Getting Started

 Salad

 Serves 4

 Total time 20 minutes

1 tablespoon **vegetable oil**
3 large boneless **chicken breasts**
¼ cup **soy sauce**
1 head **iceberg lettuce**
1 medium **carrot**
1 can (4 ounce) **water chestnuts**
¼ cup finely chopped **green onions**
1 tablespoon **sesame oil**
2 tablespoons **rice vinegar**
1 teaspoon **chili paste** (optional)
1 tablespoon **brown sugar**
1 tablespoon extra virgin **olive oil**
1 cup crispy **chow mein noodles**
iceberg lettuce for wraps (optional)

1 Heat a nonstick skillet to medium-high and add the vegetable oil.

2 Place the chicken in the pan and cook for 2–3 minutes on each side, until lightly browned.

3 Add 1 tablespoon soy sauce and cook for 2–3 more minutes, until chicken is cooked through. Add water or reduce heat if necessary to prevent burning.

4 Let chicken cool and then slice the chicken lengthwise.

5 Wash, dry and chop lettuce and place in large salad bowl.

6 Peel the carrot and discard the peel. Then, still using the peeler, cut the carrot into thin strips.

7 Add the chicken strips, carrot strips, water chestnuts, and green onions to the bowl.

8 Mix remaining soy sauce, sesame oil, rice vinegar, chili paste, brown sugar, and extra virgin olive oil. Pour over salad.

9 Garnish with crispy chow mein noodles. Serve cold with more lettuce for wraps.

The combination of the crunchy noodles and vegetables with the moist chicken breast all covered in the sweet and tangy dressing is fantastic.

PB and J Breakfast Smoothie

Eli: In the great state of California, fresh juice places are more common than gas stations. All you need is a blender or food processor (or a tall glass, masher and lots of patience). This extremely simple shake is my personal favorite as a midday snack. Prepare this shake ahead of time, keep it cold and simply pour it into a tall glass. It can satisfy all your cravings at once: part sandwich, part fruit, part sweet tooth and all parts delicious.

Getting Started

 Snack

 Serves 1–2

 Total time 10 minutes

2 cups vanilla **soy milk** or **whole milk**
⅓ cup **blueberry** or other **fruit jam**
2 whole **bananas** (preferably peeled and frozen)
⅓ cup smooth **peanut butter**
5 **ice cubes** (if using unfrozen bananas)

Combine all the ingredients in a blender and mix on high for 1–2 minutes until it reaches the consistency of a milkshake and all fruit is blended.

Variations
Add your favorite fruit.
Add a dollop of honey.
Add a teaspoon of cinnamon.

 Smoothie Tip: Keep a bag of peeled frozen bananas in your freezer and you will never have to wait in line for a smoothie again.

Gazpacho

1 large clove **garlic**
½ cup diced **green pepper**, ½-inch pieces
1 can (28 ounce) whole peeled **tomatoes**
2 cups diced **cucumber**, ½-inch pieces
1 cup diced **red onion**, ½-inch pieces
1 ½ cups diced **tomato**, ½-inch pieces
salt and **pepper** to taste
1 tablespoon finely chopped **chives**
sour cream

No heat and your guests were expecting soup? Pull the neat little gazpacho trick — a cold soup that will clear the sinuses.

Gazpacho should not be thick like salsa but it also shouldn't be thin like tomato juice either. Finding the perfect blend of veggies and the perfect consistency is the real art of gazpacho.

1 Put the garlic, green pepper, and can of whole tomatoes in the food processor or blender and blend until smooth.

2 Combine processed ingredients with remaining ingredients.

3 Add salt and pepper to taste.

4 Serve by placing in a bowl, sprinkling chives and placing a dollop of sour cream on top.

Smoked Salmon and Dill Cream Cheese Spread

Getting Started

 Appetizer

 Serves 4

 Total time 10 minutes

8 ounces **cream cheese**
3 ounces **smoked salmon**
½ tablespoon finely chopped fresh **dill**

Having all of our family in Michigan means that we've had many-a-Sunday brunch at our aunt's. From this chapter, make the tuna, the beet and cucumber dish and the summer vegetable salad. Pick up some fresh bagels, make these spreads and your brunch is ready to go. If you are of age, mimosas couldn't hurt either.

1   Place the cream cheese in a bowl and allow it to soften at room temperature.

2   Dice the smoked salmon and dill and add to the cream cheese.

3   Mix well. Serve immediately or return to refrigerator before serving.

 $ Saver Tip: Smoked salmon is expensive, and this spread is a trick I learned while cooking at a summer camp to make a little go a long way. Spread some on a bagel or a piece of toast for breakfast, along with some red onion, tomato, and cucumber slices.

Green Olive
Cream Cheese Spread

Getting Started

Appetizer

Serves 4

Total time here

8 ounces **cream cheese**

½ cup **green olives**

1 Place the cream cheese in a bowl and allow to soften at room temperature.

2 Dice the green olives and then add to the bowl.

3 Mix well. Serve immediately or return to refrigerator before serving.

Eli: The cool thing about Caprese Salad is, when you make it in your home, it tastes the same as it does in Italy. Having been to Italy several times, I have eaten my fair share of this salad and while our pasta dishes are near perfection, our Caprese is spot on.

Caprese Salad

2 ripe **tomatoes**

½ pound fresh **mozzarella cheese**

¼ pound fresh **basil**

salt and **pepper** to taste

2 tablespoons extra virgin **olive oil**

1 tablespoon **balsamic vinegar**

1 Cut tomatoes and cheese in ½-inch slices.

2 Pick the basil leaves from the stem, rinse and pat dry.

3 On a serving platter or plate, lay cheese on top of tomato, then lay basil leaf on top of cheese.

4 Repeat, using all of tomato and cheese.

5 Sprinkle lightly with salt and pepper.

6 Drizzle with olive oil and balsamic vinegar.

Beet and Cucumber Dill Salad

Remember those pesky beets your parents always wanted you to try? They're back and this time around give 'em a shot.

Getting Started

 Salad

 Serves 2

 Total time 10 minutes

1 can (12 ounce) sliced large **beets**
½ **cucumber**, peeled and sliced thin
salt and **pepper** to taste
1 tablespoon **olive oil**
1 tablespoon finely chopped fresh **dill**

1   Open the can of beets and drain the liquid.

2   Clean, peel and slice the cucumber.

3   On a serving dish, placing them in rows, alternate the beet slice and cucumber slice.

4   Season with salt and pepper to taste.

5   Drizzle the entire plate with the olive oil, sprinkle the entire dish with the chopped dill and serve.

Variation

Fennel: Replace the dill with chopped fennel leaves for a slightly different, licorice-type flavor.

Michigan Chicken Salad

When people ask where we are from we do say Detroit, but we are really from the 'burbs. The hardcore 'burbs though, and we ALWAYS keep it real. Being from Michigan we had to incorporate a little salute to the "mitten" state with this classy take on chicken salad. Getting dried cherries all the way from Traverse City, Michigan may seem grandiosely ostentatious (like my computer's thesaurus function) but in the end it's all about the flavor.

Getting Started

 Salad / Main Course

 Serves 4–6

 Total time 30 minutes

3 large boneless **chicken breasts**
3 tablespoons extra virgin **olive oil**
¼ cup **lemon juice**
½ cup Michigan **dried cherries**
10 large **walnuts**, coarsely chopped
2 stalks diced **celery**, ½-inch pieces
½ cup **mayonnaise**
2 tablespoons **garlic powder**
1 tablespoon dried **dill**
½ cup **green grapes**, sliced lengthwise
salt and **pepper** to taste

1 In a large skillet, place the chicken, olive oil, and lemon juice. Bring to a simmer and cook until chicken is done, about 10–15 minutes. Add water and/or reduce heat to prevent burning if necessary. Remove chicken from heat and set aside.

2 While the chicken is cooking, combine cherries, walnuts, and celery in a large bowl.

3 When chicken is cooked and cooled slightly, dice to ½-inch.

4 Add chicken, mayonnaise, garlic powder and dill to the mixing bowl and mix well.

5 Add the grapes and gently mix in.

6 Season with salt and pepper to taste.

7 Serve cold by itself, with crackers or as a sandwich.

 Timesaver: This recipe uses chicken breasts instead of canned chicken (like I would use for tuna salad). To make this recipe faster and with fewer steps, you can use canned chicken breast meat. If you choose to do that, use around 3–4 cans (20 ounce size).

Guacamole

3 ripe **avocadoes**

2 tablespoons **lemon juice**

2 tablespoons minced **garlic**

2 tablespoons (tightly packed) chopped **cilantro**

1 teaspoon ground **cumin** (optional)

¼ cup diced **tomato**, ½-inch pieces

¼ cup diced **onion**, ¼-inch pieces

salt to taste

Max: When I was in high school I came up with a scheme to make guacamole and sell it in stores. I perfected my recipe, "borrowed" some small plastic containers from the health food store where I worked, and designed a logo. The name I came up with was "The Best Guacamole You Will Ever Have In the Universe." This plan never got off the ground, but at least now you have the recipe.

1. Peel the avocadoes and remove pit.

2. Mash the avocadoes using a potato masher or fork.

3. Add the lemon juice, garlic, cilantro, cumin (if using), and salt; mix well.

4. Add tomato and onion and mix gently.

5. Let sit for 20 minutes for flavors to blend together.

Fresh tip: Leaving the pit in the guacamole will help preserve it longer.

Homemade Hummus with Toasted Pita Triangles

Max: If you've never had hummus, you are missing out. This flavorful dip can be used on sandwiches or on its own with some carrots or pita to dip. Here we have livened up some store-bought pita bread by toasting it with olive oil and garlic. Homemade Hummus is a little different than the store-bought variety. It is a little chunkier, but it doesn't get any fresher than this.

If you're out of pita or crave some veggies, cut up some celery, red pepper, and carrots into sticks and dip them in the Hummus.

Getting Started

 Appetizer

 Serves 4

 Total time 10 minutes

1 can (15 ounce) **chickpeas** (garbanzo beans)
1–2 cloves minced **garlic**
2 tablespoons extra virgin **olive oil**
2 tablespoons **lemon juice**
¼ cup **water**
3 tablespoons **tahini** (sesame paste), available at Middle-East markets and many supermarkets
water, if needed
salt to taste
Toasted **Pita Triangles**, recipe follows

1. Drain the chickpeas and reserve the liquid.

2. In a food processor, blend the chickpeas and garlic, adding the olive oil slowly.

3. Add the lemon juice, tahini, water, and enough of the chickpea liquid until mixture reaches a smooth, thick consistency. Add more water if needed.

4. Season with salt to taste.

5. Serve with Toasted Pita Triangles.

Variations

Roasted Red Pepper: Add 2 tablespoons Roasted Red Pepper, page 130, at the beginning, and reduce water to 1 teaspoon.

Spicy: Add 1 teaspoon crushed red chili peppers.

Pine Nut: Sprinkle 2 tablespoons toasted pine nuts over the top before serving.

Zatar and Sesame Seed: Sprinkle 1 teaspoon Zatar (a Middle-Eastern spice) and 1 teaspoon toasted sesame seeds over the top.

Toasted Pita Triangles

Appetizer

Serves 4

Total time here

1 package **pita bread**
¼ cup **olive oil**
1 teaspoon **garlic powder**

1 Preheat oven to 275°F.

2 Cut pita bread into wedges.

3 Brush lightly with olive oil.

4 Sprinkle lightly with garlic powder.

5 Place on cookie sheet in oven for 10 minutes or until golden brown and crunchy.

Summer Vegetable Salad

This salad is a triple treat: it's fresh, fast and delicious. For a vegetarian or someone looking for a healthy alternative, this salad can be your go-to lunch. If you want some more flavor-action think about adding some cheddar cheese cubes, tuna or diced chicken breast.

For salads, we like to make our own dressings. Most store-bought dressings are loaded with fat, artificial ingredients and mask the great flavor the salad provides. A dressing made from extra virgin olive oil and balsamic vinegar with salt, pepper and garlic allows the flavor of the vegetables to come through.

Getting Started

 Salad / Main Course

 Serves 4

 Total time 20 minutes

1 can (8 ounce) **sweet corn**

1 can (8 ounce) **chickpeas** (garbanzo beans)

½ head romaine **lettuce leaves**, coarsely chopped

1 **carrot**, washed, peeled, and chopped

1 diced **celery stalk**, ½-inch pieces

1 diced **cucumber**, ¼-inch pieces

1 diced **red onion**, ¼-inch pieces

1 **tomato**, chopped

3 tablespoon **olive oil**

2 tablespoons **balsamic vinegar**

1 clove **garlic** minced, or 1 teaspoon **garlic powder**

1 teaspoon dried **thyme**

salt and **pepper** to taste

¼ cup **sunflower seeds**

1. Open and drain the corn and chickpeas, and pour into a large mixing bowl.

2. Add the lettuce, carrot, celery, cucumber, red onion, tomato, and add to the bowl.

3. Mix the olive oil, balsamic vinegar, garlic or garlic powder, thyme, and salt and pepper in a separate bowl.

4. Pour the dressing over the salad and toss lightly.

5. Sprinkle the sunflower seeds on top and serve.

Tip: Here is a tip to use during the summer when fresh sweet corn is abundant. Its fresh flavor can't be beat! Instead of the can of corn, take 2–3 cobs of shucked sweet corn. Stand the corn sticking straight up and hold it at the tip. Then, using a chef's knife, carefully slice down the length of the corn, just deep enough to slice off the kernels. Rotate the corn and repeat until all kernels are removed. Then dunk in boiling water for 1 minute. Immediately remove and place in ice water to cool. Drain and add to salad in step 1.

Tomato, Onion, and Cucumber Salad

Getting Started

Salad

Serves 2

Total time 10 minutes

1 large diced **tomato**, ½-inch pieces
1 diced **cucumber**, ½-inch pieces
¼ cup diced **onion**, ½-inch pieces
2 tablespoons **olive oil**
1 tablespoon **lemon juice**
salt and **pepper** to taste

This salad is so great because it's simple. Only a few ingredients and the right touch of a light dressing keeps the flavor focus of the salad exactly where it should be — on the veggies.

1   Mix together tomato, cucumber, onion, olive oil, and lemon juice.

2   Season with salt and pepper to taste and serve.

Tuna Salad

Eli: This deli-style tuna recipe single-handedly sustained me through college. While the smell of tuna might be too strong for the close quarters you share with your roommate, classmate or coworker, you can't deny its stellar taste. For the healthy living set, cut the mayonnaise serving in half and squeeze a little fresh lemon juice into the mix for flavor.

Getting Started

 Salad

 Serves 2

 Total time 10 minutes

2 cans (6 ounces each) **tuna fish**, drained

3–4 tablespoons famous brand tangy **mayonnaise**

¼ teaspoon **pepper**

2 pinches **garlic powder**

2 pinches **salt**

1 **celery stalk**, sliced lengthwise and then diced, ¼-inch pieces

¼ diced **red onion**, ¼-inch pieces

1 **pickle** spear, diced, ¼-inch pieces (optional)

1 teaspoon finely chopped fresh **dill**

1 **lemon** (optional)

1 Empty tuna into a large bowl. Break up large chunks with a fork.

2 Add the mayonnaise and mix well.

3 Add the pepper, garlic powder and salt. Mix well.

4 Add the celery, dill and pickle (if using). Mix gently. Add freshly squeezed lemon or serve wedge on the side. Serve cold.

Variations

Tuna Melt: Take two slices of bread and spread butter on one side of each. Place tuna salad, a slice of tomato and a slice of sharp cheddar cheese on the side without butter. Close the sandwich so that the butter is facing out on both slices. Cook in a nonstick frying pan on medium-low heat until bread in golden brown and cheese is melted, about 3-4 minutes on each side.

Trail Mix

Going on a hike? Going canoeing? Going to sit around and watch TV all day? Make this. Eat it. Be very happy.

This recipe is great for a tailgate, camping, a long drive or just for snacking. If you are going to keep this in the sun or it's a hot day you might want to leave out the chocolate chips.

Getting Started

Snack

Serves 4–6

Total time 5 minutes

1 cup honey roasted **peanuts**

½ cup **sunflower seeds**

1 cup famous brand O **cereal**

½ cup dried **cranberries**

½ cup **almonds**

½ cup **cashews**

½ cup **chocolate chips**

Combine all ingredients.

Heat

By osmosis or sheer luck, you learned a long time ago in a very boring class that once cavemen figured out fire, everything really started to pick up. It was fire on Monday, the wheel on Tuesday and fast-food, internet and pausing live TV soon after that. Fire changed everything for cavemen and learning how to properly use your oven or heat source can change cooking for you.

Anyone that knows us well will tell you that we are extremely manly men. Building shelters and wielding an ax is second nature to us. The whole hunter routine doesn't scare us, but the thought of having to eat uncooked wooly mammoth doesn't exactly excite us. Using your stove and frying pan is a good thing and we plan to teach you how.

This chapter we begin to focus on recipes that use heat as an integral part of the cooking process. We know you may never have ventured further past a microwave burrito, but we will bring you along slowly. This is one of those crawl before you run routines because anyone knows that running with fire is extremely dangerous. Even a caveman can figure that out.

If some cooks believe cooking with a lot of rosemary is a crime...then lock us up. This dish combines some of our favorite earthly delights. Whether you are into creationism or science there is no debate that combining potatoes, garlic, rosemary and extra virgin olive oil are matches made in heaven (or some scientifically accepted afterlife, or not at all depending on what you believe). Whatever you do is cool, we won't judge.

Roasted Rosemary Potatoes

Heat

Side Dish

Serves 2

Total time 30 minutes

2 tablespoons **blended oil**

2 cups diced Idaho **potatoes**, ½-inch pieces

1 tablespoon finely chopped fresh **rosemary**

6 cloves **garlic**, cut in half if very large

salt and **pepper**

1 In a medium sized nonstick skillet, heat the oil over medium heat.

2 When the oil begins to shimmer and sizzle, add the potatoes. If you are not using a nonstick skillet, quickly shake the pan a few times to prevent them from sticking.

3 Cook for about 10 minutes, until just beginning to brown, stirring frequently.

4 Add rosemary and cook until nearly done, about 10–15 more minutes.

5 Add garlic and cook for 5 more minutes.

6 Season with salt and pepper to taste.

Kitchen Tip: Blended Oil Some recipes call for blended oil. This is a restaurant trick to get some of the good flavor of olive oil without the high price tag. Adding vegetable or canola oil to extra virgin olive oil also raises the smoking point, so you can sauté at high heat and still keep some of the olive oil flavor. The ratio should be 1:1 for the vegetable/canola oil to olive oil.

How to Boil Pasta

We promised to teach you how to boil pasta, so here it is. For those of you who love the details, we are happy to indulge.

Make sure you use a big enough pot. If you see your pasta poking out above the water as it cooks, you need more water.

Add salt to the boiling water. This will give some flavor to the pasta itself.

On the pasta box, it will say how long to cook the pasta. Set a timer for the low end of the time range, and taste the pasta when the timer goes off. The pasta should be cooked "al dente," meaning tender and chewy, just past crunchy and before mushy. Taste a noodle and if it is still crunchy, it needs more time, but if it bounces back slightly when you bite into it, it's ready .

When the pasta is done, don't leave it in the hot water! Drain it immediately, but don't rinse it. When you rinse pasta you remove the starch that your sauce or dressing loves to cling to and makes each bite even more delicious.

Shake the colander (that's a strainer, folks) until no more water comes out. Immediately add some butter or extra virgin olive oil and a dash of salt (depending on the recipe!). Toss the pasta well. If the butter is cold, cut it into a few pieces so it melts evenly through the pasta. This step is what prevents your pasta from sticking into a tangled mess 10 minutes later.

Enjoy your perfectly prepared, delicious, al dente pasta!

Mediterranean Pasta Salad

Pasta is cheap, filling, and delicious. If you're on a budget, learning how to dress up pasta is a skill worth learning. This pasta salad can be as light or as filling as you wish. By adding more cheese or sliced chicken breast it becomes enough to serve as an entrée — toasted pita on the side!

Heat

Pasta Salad

Serves 4

Total time 30 minutes

Kosher salt

½ red **onion**, thinly sliced

8 ounces dry multi-color spiral or penne **pasta**

5 tablespoons extra virgin **olive oil**

4 ounces **sun-dried tomatoes**

1 large diced **cucumber**, ½-inch pieces

1 large diced **red pepper**, ½-inch pieces

½ large diced **green pepper**, ½-inch pieces

8 ounces pitted **Kalamata olives**

6 ounces crumbled **feta cheese**

1 tablespoon **oregano**

1 teaspoon **basil**

1 tablespoon **garlic powder**

salt and **pepper** to taste

2 tablespoons **Parmesan cheese**

1. Lightly sprinkle some kosher salt over the sliced onions and let them rest in a colander while the pasta cooks (this takes some of the harshness out of the onions).

2. Cook pasta according to directions on the box. Drain pasta, toss with 2 tablespoons olive oil and set aside. Allow to cool to room temperature before mixing with other ingredients.

3. Place remaining ingredients except Parmesan cheese in large bowl and mix well.

4. Taste and adjust salt and pepper if needed.

5. Top with Parmesan cheese.

Serving note: If you don't serve this immediately, keep the cheese and cucumbers out until right before serving. Allowing this pasta salad to marinate over night allows the flavor of the dressing to get into the pasta and veggies. If you have time, it is suggested.

Sweet and Sour Meatballs

Eli: I know what you are thinking. Sweet AND sour? At the same time? Welcome to the future where you can time travel by driving a Delorean 88 miles per hour through downtown Main Street.

And whosever idea it was to shrink meatballs down to bite size is a genius. So far no one has really taken credit for it on Wikipedia and I want credit for it. Ok, you know what, I am taking it. Credit for baby meatballs is officially mine.

Heat

 Main Course

 Serves 4

Total time 40 minutes

½ pound ground **pork**

½ pound ground **beef**

2 tablespoons **breadcrumbs**

1 tablespoon minced **garlic**

1 teaspoon minced **ginger**

1 teaspoon **chili sauce** or ½ teaspoon **cayenne pepper**

salt and **pepper** to taste

3 tablespoons **vegetable oil**

¼ cup **onion** or **shallot**, minced, divided

½ cup **mirin** (sweet rice wine)

1 cup **chicken broth**

¼ cup **fruit jam** (preferably **orange marmalade**)

¼ cup **white vinegar**

2 teaspoon **cornstarch**

3 tablespoons **water**

Basmati Rice, page 91

1. Mix together ground pork, ground beef, breadcrumbs, garlic, half the ginger, chili sauce or cayenne pepper, and salt and pepper to taste.

2. Form into ¾-inch meatballs. You should have about 25–30. Set aside.

3. Heat 1 tablespoon oil to medium-high in a medium size pot.

4. Add the onion or shallot and remaining ginger and sauté for 4–5 minutes.

5. Add the wine and cook for 3–4 minutes.

6. Add the chicken broth, jam, and vinegar and bring to a simmer.

7. Dissolve 2 teaspoons cornstarch in 3 tablespoons of water in a bowl.

8. Add mixture to the sauce and continue to simmer on low. Sauce will begin to thicken.

9. Heat 2 tablespoons oil in a nonstick skillet.

10. Add the meatballs and cook on medium-high, turning until they are browned on all surfaces. You may have to do this in two batches.

11. As the meatballs brown, gently place them in the simmering sauce.

12. Simmer for 10–15 minutes and serve with Basmati Rice.

Baby Meatballs

Heat

Main Course

Serves 4–6

Prep Time 20 minutes/Total time 50 minutes

1 pound fresh **ground beef**

2 tablespoons **oregano**

¼ cup Italian **breadcrumbs** or **Homemade Breadcrumbs**, page 128

¼ cup **ricotta cheese**

1 minced **garlic** clove or 1 tablespoon **garlic powder**

2 tablespoons grated **Parmesan cheese**

1 jar **tomato sauce** (24 ounces) or 1 batch **Homemade Marinara Sauce**, page 145

1   Mix meat with oregano, breadcrumbs, ricotta cheese, garlic, and Parmesan cheese.

2   Form the meat into roughly ping-pong sized balls.

3   Place meatballs in pot on medium heat, leaving at least ½-inch of space between each meatball.

4   When the meatball begins to brown, after about 1–2 minutes, gently turn each ball. Repeat until meatballs are browned on all sides.

5   Add the Marinara Sauce, cover and simmer for 25–30 minutes, stirring occasionally.

6   Remove meatballs from sauce with a slotted spoon if you have one and arrange on a serving dish. Try to keep the majority of the sauce in the pot.

7   Sprinkle with Parmesan cheese.

8   Serve immediately with the sauce in a side dish for dipping.

Cooking Basics

Sauté

When you cook something in a hot pan with a small amount of oil, you are sautéing. If you've done this before, you may have not known that there was a fancy French word for what you were doing!

For a great sauté, heat a pan for a few minutes with nothing at all in it. Then add a few tablespoons of oil or butter. Add your meat or vegetables and make sure not to crowd the pan. You want the food you're cooking in contact with the heat of the oil, and if you add too much to the pan you will be creating steam, which means that you won't get that lovely brown color.

Roasting

Roasting in the oven has a lot of similarities to sautéing. You want to use a light but thorough coating of oil and you don't want to crowd your dish. Steam is your enemy! If you use too many potatoes, you won't get that nice crisp golden brown edge on the outside.

Baking

The oven is your friend. Learn to use the oven. Nowhere else can you make such a wide range of dishes from casseroles to cakes.

Here are some pointers to achieve best results every time you put something in the oven.

• Make sure you oven is preheated. If your oven takes 15 minutes to preheat, and the recipe says to bake for 20 minutes, then your dish spent over half the cooking time at the wrong temperature. That will definitely affect whatever you're making.

• Try not to open the oven door until you really need to. Most recipes give a time range of when your dish will be ready. Each time you open the door, the oven can lose 10 or 20 degrees. The front of the oven will be even cooler than the back, and certain things like muffins and cakes might deflate. Bad news!

• Rotate your cookies, and anything else, especially if you have an older oven. Most ovens are hotter in the back so if you're baking for a long time, 20 minutes or more, at a hot temperature, you will want to rotate your tray halfway through.

Homemade Fresh Tomato Salsa

Heat

Side Dish

Serves 4

Total time 20 minutes

3 tablespoons extra virgin **olive oil**

1 large diced **green pepper**, ½-inch pieces

1 large diced **red pepper**, ½-inch pieces

1 diced medium **red onion**, ¼-inch pieces

1 **jalapeño pepper** minced

1 large **garlic** clove, minced

1 large diced **tomato**, ½-inch pieces

2 tablespoons finely chopped **cilantro**

This is a "garden-style" recipe for salsa with chunky vegetables and a bit of kick to it. A variation is to not cook any of the vegetables. Just dice, mix and serve while keeping it all cold and crunchy. This salsa, served with chips and Guacamole (page 37) is a must for any party, tailgate or TV watching event. Throw some cheese and/or chicken into this chip-dip equation and you've got yourself a meal.

Making salsa using fresh ingredients makes a serious difference when you go for the dip. You've got chunks of veggies, not some store bought mess. The fresh flavors will jump out at you and you will be sad to see this salsa go.

1   Heat the olive oil in a large skillet until shimmering.

2   Add the peppers, onions and jalapeños and cook on medium heat for 5 minutes.

3   Add the garlic and cook on medium heat for 2 minutes.

4   Remove the skillet from the heat. Place all the vegetables in a dish and allow to cool 30 minutes or until room temperature.

5   Add the tomatoes and cliantro and mix thoroughly.

53

French Toast

 Main Course

 Serves 4–6

 Total time 30 minutes

Heat

1 loaf **challah**
6 **eggs**
1 cup heavy **cream**
2 tablespoons **sugar**
1 teaspoon **cinnamon** (optional)
2 tablespoons **oil** plus more as needed
maple syrup and **powdered sugar**

Max: As Max Biyalistock in Mel Brooks' The Producers *said, "When you got it baby, flaunt it!" Well this recipe's got it. Use a loaf of day old challah and slice it into nice thick slices so it can absorb the egg and cream custard. This French toast is a picture of golden brown perfection. One bite and you will never skip breakfast again — irresistible by itself or when complemented by some boysenberry jam, maple syrup or chocolate spread.*

1   Slice the challah to 1 ½-inch thick slices.

2   Mix the eggs, cream, sugar, and cinnamon in a flat container with 2-inch or higher sides. Try to use a container that can fit at least 2 pieces of challah at a time.

3   Soak challah for 5–10 minutes each side (yes, it takes that long).

4   Heat a skillet to medium heat and add oil.

5   Cook challah for 3–4 minutes on each side until golden brown. Don't rush it!

6   Pour maple syrup and shake powdered sugar, if desired.

Breakfast Savory Potatoes

Max: Sunday potluck brunches have become something of a tradition at my house. We invite over all our friends for around 11 in the morning. Everyone ends up standing in the kitchen helping and snacking, and usually we're still cooking until about 1PM. These potatoes have been refined and tested over many of these brunches and are one of the first things to disappear once we 'start' eating. I have been known to use lots of dishes when I cook, but in this case it's worth it.

Heat

Side Dish

Serves 2

Total time 25 minutes

2–3 large **potatoes** (enough to yield 2 cups when diced)

1 teaspoon **salt**

5 tablespoons **blended oil**, page 47

½ cup diced **onion**, ¼-inch pieces

½ cup diced **green pepper**, ¼-inch pieces

1 teaspoon minced **garlic**

2 teaspoons dried **thyme**

1 tablespoon **paprika**

1 tablespoon **Herb Butter**, page 126 (optional)

salt and **pepper** to taste

1 Wash and dice the potatoes to ½-inch. Place in a pot and cover with water and 1 teaspoon salt.

2 Bring potatoes and water to a boil. As soon as the water boils, drain the potatoes well and pat dry with paper towel.

3 Heat the oil in two pans, 3 tablespoons in one and 2 in the other. When the oil begins to shimmer and sizzle, add the diced potatoes in one (larger if the pans are different sizes) and the onion and green peppers in the other.

4 Sauté for 10 minutes, or until potatoes are golden and crispy on the outside, and tender and cooked through on the inside. The green peppers and onions should be very soft.

5 Add the garlic, thyme, and paprika to the green pepper and onions and sauté for 2–3 more minutes. Mix together.

6 Stir in Herb Butter (if using) and salt and pepper to taste and serve.

Flavor tip: For extra crispy potatoes, instead of cooking in a pan, toss in a bowl with oil, thyme, paprika, salt, and pepper, and cook on a baking sheet in a preheated oven at 425°F until browned, moving the potatoes around with spatula occasionally, about 15 minutes.

Mom's Style "Goulash"

Goulash is a traditional Hungarian dish that has a cut of meat stewed in a broth with lots of paprika. American versions of goulash tend to add tomato sauce and cut down on the paprika. This version is a cross between a traditional version and an American version; it still has lots of paprika flavor but also tomatoes and ground beef.

Heat

 Main Course

 Serves 4–6

 Total time 30 minutes

3 tablespoons extra virgin **olive oil**

1 medium diced **onion**, ½-inch pieces

3 minced cloves of **garlic**

1 pound lean **ground beef**

1 can (28 ounce) crushed **tomatoes**

2 tablespoons **tomato paste**

1 cup **chicken broth**

4 tablespoons **paprika**

1 pound dry penne **pasta**

hot sauce or **chili sauce** (optional)

1. Heat 1 tablespoon olive oil in a thick-bottomed soup pot or Dutch oven until shimmering.

2. Add onions and cook on medium until soft, 4–5 minutes.

3. Add garlic and cook for another minute.

4. Remove garlic and onions and set aside.

5. Heat 1 tablespoon olive oil and add ground beef.

6. Continue to cook beef, stirring regularly, until browned.

7. Add crushed tomatoes, tomato paste, chicken broth, cooked garlic and onions, and 3 tablespoons paprika; reduce heat to low and simmer for 20 minutes.

8. While sauce is simmering, cook pasta according to directions on the box. Drain pasta, toss with last tablespoon olive oil and set aside.

9. When sauce is ready, add pasta and cook for 1 minute more. Remove from heat and stir in remaining paprika. Serve with hot sauce on the side.

Nana's Cheesy Scalloped Potatoes

Heat

Side Dish

Serves 4–6

Prep Time 15 minutes/Total time (including baking) 1 hour

2 pounds thinly sliced **Idaho potatoes**

1 medium **onion**, diced to ¼-inch

1 clove **garlic**, minced

3 tablespoons **butter**

2 tablespoons **flour**

1 ½ cups grated sharp **cheddar cheese**

¾ cup warm **milk**

salt and **pepper**

This is our Nana's delicious recipe. Our family is huge into the Sunday brunch and we have been eating this for years. It's fast and easy, just put it in the oven and enjoy!

1 Preheat oven to 375°F and place oven rack in top section of the oven.

2 Coat the sides of a 13 x 9 baking pan with the butter. You will have extra butter. Set it aside.

3 Toss potatoes, onions, garlic, flour, half the cheese and generous amount of salt and pepper. Mix very well so that everything is evenly distributed and you can't see the flour anymore, then pour into buttered baking dish.

4 Break up the butter into small pieces with your hands and place them evenly spaced over the potatoes.

5 Pour milk over, then sprinkle remaining cheese on top of that.

6 Cover with foil and bake 15 minutes.

7 Uncover and continue cooking until potatoes are soft and cheese is brown and bubbly, 20–30 minutes longer.

Potato Leek Soup

This soup, like Mushroom Barley Soup, opposite, lets just a few simple ingredients shine. You can skip the cream, but we suggest leaving it in for a heartier wintertime soup.

Heat

 Soup

 Serves 2–3

 Prep Time 15 minutes/Total time 1 hour

3 tablespoons **butter** or extra virgin **olive oil**

2–3 bunches **leeks** (washed carefully to remove sand)

½ cup **white wine** (optional)

2 diced medium **potatoes**, ½-inch pieces (peeled or unpeeled, your preference)

1 teaspoon dried **thyme**

8 cups **vegetable** or **chicken broth**

1 cup **half and half** or **heavy cream** (optional)

salt and **pepper**

1 Thinly slice leeks crosswise (see Cleaning Leeks, below). Start at the white end, discarding the very end, and move towards green part. Don't use the darker green parts that are tough.

2 Heat the butter or olive oil in a large pot.

3 Add the leeks to the pot and sauté until soft, about 5 minutes.

4 Add the white wine if using and simmer until liquid is gone, about 5–7 minutes.

5 Add potatoes, thyme and broth and simmer until potatoes are tender, about 20–30 minutes.

6 Add half and half or cream if using and salt and pepper to taste.

Kitchen Technique: Cleaning Leeks Leeks' subtle yet unmistakable flavor is wonderful, yet they can be quite dirty on the inside. To clean leeks, first cut off the darker green sections, and then slice the lighter section lengthwise. Remove the very bottom with the roots, then soak in a pot of cold water for 5 minutes, moving the leeks around occasionally. The dirt should sink to the bottom and you can remove your cleaned leeks. If necessary, drain the water and clean again.

Mushroom Barley Soup

Heat

Soup

Serves 6–8

Prep time 20 minutes/Total time 50 minutes

1–2 ounces dried **porcini mushrooms,** ½-inch pieces (optional)

6 ounces fresh **button mushrooms**

2 stalks diced **celery**, ½-inch pieces

2–3 diced **carrots**, ¾-inch pieces

1 diced medium **onion**, ½-inch pieces

3 tablespoons **butter**

2 medium diced **potatoes**, ¾-inch pieces

¾ cup **pearl barley**

2–3 cups **vegetable stock**

2–3 cups **mushroom stock**

salt and **pepper** to taste

This is our Nana's recipe, and it is often served when our family gets together. It's always a big hit. When she sent us the recipe, we saw that the secret was its simplicity. Take note readers, the best recipes often use just a few simple, fresh ingredients — let them be the star of the show. Splurge on some dried porcini mushrooms to intensify the flavor.

1 Re-hydrate the dried mushrooms by soaking in enough warm water to cover until soft. Strain through a fine-mesh sieve, reserving the liquid, and set aside.

2 Sauté the mushrooms, celery, carrots, and onion in butter in a large soup pan until soft.

3 Add potatoes, barley, reserved mushroom liquid, and stock. Bring to a boil, then lower heat and cook slowly until flavors blend and soup thickens. If it thickens too much, more broth can be added.

Grilled Ham
and Cheese

Heat

 Main Course

 Serves 1

Total time 10 minutes

So you have tried to make grilled ham and cheese before and you burned your bread or the cheese wasn't melted. Well, follow our directions here and you'll never have that problem again. It is one of those magical combinations that will last for all of eternity because ham and cheese can be a cheap eat. In so many incarnations — from one piece of ham and one piece of cheese to an overflowing sandwich with different fine cheese varieties, oozing over a nice stack of smoked ham — so tasty.

This sandwich is really simple to make. It comes out great in a skillet or on a celebrity grill.

2 pieces large **Texas toast** or **thick bread**
2 tablespoons **butter**, at room temperature
3 slices **ham**
2 slices **cheese**, your choice

Directions for skillet

1 Gently spread the butter evenly on the toast.

2 Place the bread butter side down in the skillet on the stove.

3 Place one piece of cheese on each slice of bread.

4 Heat the bread for 2 minutes and then add ham.

5 When the underside of the bread becomes a golden brown (you can peek underneath, it's ok), place the other piece of bread over the ham, butter side up, and flip.

6 Cook for another 2 minutes and then eat.

Directions for celebrity grill

1 Butter one side of each piece of bread.

2 On the non-butter side put the cheese and meat.

3 Close the sandwich so that both buttered sides face out.

4 Put the sandwich on the celebrity grill and close, heat on medium for 2 minutes.

Microwave Buffalo Chicken Wrap

Heat

Main Course

Serves 1

Time 10 minutes

1 tablespoon extra virgin **olive oil**

1 **chicken breast**

1 flour **tortilla**

2 slices **tomato**

¼ cup shredded **lettuce**

1 tablespoon **Ranch Dressing**

Frank's Red Hot sauce

2 tablespoons diced **red onion**, ¼-inch pieces

1 tablespoon diced **bacon**, ½-inch pieces

¼ cup shredded **Mexican cheese** blend (optional)

Eli: This dish is a micro adaptation of a favorite of the staff of the restaurant where I worked during college. It wasn't on the menu but if you knew the right people and the right way to ask for it, you could be part of the exclusive club that could order this sandwich.

1 Spread olive oil evenly over chicken breast on a microwave-proof plate. Microwave on high until chicken is cooked through, about 2–4 minutes.

2 Cut chicken into ½-inch cubes. If the middle of the chicken is not fully cooked, replace uncooked pieces in microwave for 20–30 seconds. Make sure to evenly cover the pieces in a small amount of olive oil so the chicken does not dry out.

3 Assemble the sandwich by placing ingredients in the following order on the tortilla: tomato, lettuce, chicken, Ranch Dressing, hot sauce, red onion, and bacon. Roll up the tortilla placing the folded side down on a clean plate.

4 If you wish, sprinkle cheese on top and return to microwave on high for 30 seconds.

5 Cut in half and serve.

Microwave Mashed Potatoes

Eli : Mashed potatoes in the microwave are faster and easier than mashed potatoes any other way. Keep everything in the same plastic dish and then keep the leftovers in the exact same micro safe dish to store them for tomorrow. Gotta love that plastic. Thanks, science! Need to heat 'em up? Back into the micro. Thanks again, science! You're the best! Text me sometime! We should hang out!

Heat

 Side Dish

 Serves 4

 Total time 15 minutes

5 large **Idaho potatoes**, peeled
1 large **microwave safe dish** that can fit the potatoes
4 tablespoons **butter** or **margarine**
½ cup **half and half** or **whole milk**
salt and **pepper**, to taste
1 clove minced **garlic** or 1 teaspoon **garlic powder**

1 Cut each potato into 6 equal pieces. Place in microwave-safe dish filled with water to cover potatoes.

2 Cook on high, covered for 8 minutes.

3 Take a fork and cut one piece of potato into smaller pieces. If this is still difficult, put back in microwave on high for 2 more minutes.

4 Remove dish from microwave, drain water but keep potatoes in dish.

5 Mash potatoes using a masher, fork or anything in your kitchen drawer that mashes well.

6 Add butter or margarine and mix well. Add the milk or half and half slowly while mixing it in. You may decide to not use the entire amount.

7 Season to taste with salt, pepper, garlic or garlic powder, and serve.

Timesaver: Thawing Shrimp

Place the shrimp in a colander and run cold water over the shrimp. In about 5 minutes they should be thawed.

Timesaver: Thawing Chicken

Odds are you buy frozen chicken breasts. Thawing in the fridge can take forever, and thawing at room temperature is a bad idea because salmonella will grow. Try this tip: Place chicken breasts in a bowl, and thaw them under a thin steady steam of cold running water. Thawed out chicken in no time at all.

Quick Jumble Jambalaya

Eli: This isn't your typical jambalaya. It's more of a speed version. At the deli counter at your grocery store ask for the type of sausage listed below. They should have it, but if not, just use the closest thing you can find. Frozen shrimp with the tail on is cheaper but don't forget to take the tails off before you put them in!

Heat

Main Course

Serves 2

Total time 40 minutes

1½ cups **white rice**

3 tablespoons blended **olive oil**

1 diced **chicken breast**, ½-inch pieces

2 tablespoons **paprika**, divided

1 raw **Italian sausage**, sliced to ¼-inch pieces

1 can (8 ounce) of **black beans**, drained

10 **shrimp**, thawed and tails removed

salt and **pepper** to taste

---

1   Cook 1 ½ cups rice according to package directions.

2   Heat 2 tablespoons oil on medium heat.

3   Add the chicken cubes and 1 tablespoon paprika and cook on medium heat in the oil for 5 minutes stirring occasionally.

4   Remove the chicken when browned and set aside.

5   Add 1 tablespoon oil and the sausage to the pan and cook until brown all around, turning every minute or so.

6   Add the beans and chicken to the pan, and cook for 2 minutes, stirring often.

7   Add the thawed shrimp, stir in and cook for 30 seconds.

8   Add remaining paprika, salt and pepper to taste.

9   Put the cooked rice in bowls or on a plate.

10 Remove jambalaya from heat and pour over the cooked rice and serve immediately.

Potato Skins in the Microwave

A huge hit with the drinking crowd, you can crank these out in a very short time using your microwave. For parties, sports events and outdoor BBQs, your guests will eat these so fast you will start to wonder if you should have even made anything else. Remember to save the middle portion for mashed potatoes.

Heat

 Side Dish

 Serves 4

 Total time 20 minutes

4 large **potatoes**
1–2 cups **cheddar cheese**, shredded or broken into small pieces
3 tablespoons **Bacon Bits** or 3 diced cooked **bacon slices**, ¼-inch pieces
2 tablespoons thinly sliced **green onion**
garlic powder (optional)
sour cream (optional)

1. Cut potatoes into wedges, lengthwise, 2 or 4 pieces depending on the size of the potato. Place in microwave-safe dish filled with water to cover potatoes.

2. Cook on high heat for 7 minutes.

3. Remove and test for doneness by poking with a knife. If you cannot scoop out the inside of the potato, return to microwave on high for 1 minute at a time until finished.

4. Scoop out the potato so ¼-inch thickness remains around shell of potato.

5. Sprinkle cheese over the top and return to microwave for 1–2 minutes, until cheese is melted.

6. Remove and sprinkle with Bacon Bits, green onion and top with a shake of garlic powder and a dollop of sour cream, if desired.

Santa Fe Omelet

Max: When it comes to the making of an omelet, Eli and I part ways. Eli prefers to flip his omelet up in the air and I don't. Either way, a good nonstick 10-inch skillet is a crucial ingredient for this recipe. Read on below for the different ways to make an omelet. Mastering the omelet with a flip is easier said than done, but if you follow the instructions you should have it down in no time. If you mess up the flip, don't fret, just roll with it and you have a "Santa Fe Scramble," just as delicious. If you are into spicy, dice up a bit of jalapeño and put it in with all the veggies.

Heat

 Main Course

 Serves 1

 Total time 20 minutes

3 **eggs**

pinch **salt** and **pepper**

1 tablespoon extra virgin **olive oil**

¼ cup diced **red onion**, ½-inch pieces

¼ cup diced **green pepper**, ½-inch pieces

¼ cup diced **ham**, ½-inch pieces

¼ **jalapeño pepper**, de-seeded and minced (optional)

¼ cup diced **tomato**, ½-inch pieces

2 tablespoons **butter**

Tabasco (optional)

1 ounce **Cheddar cheese**, shredded

1 ounce **Monterey Jack cheese**, shredded

¼ cup store bought **salsa** or **Homemade Fresh Tomato Salsa**, page 53

1. Very lightly beat eggs, salt, and pepper in a mixing bowl, until the yolks and whites are just mixed.

2. Heat 1 tablespoon olive oil in a nonstick skillet on medium heat.

3. Add red onion, green pepper, ham, and jalapeño (if using) to the skillet and cook 3–5 minutes, or until onions are translucent. Add tomatoes and cook for 1 minute longer.

4. Remove the vegetables, set aside and wipe out the pan with paper towel or kitchen towel.

5. Reheat the empty skillet on medium-low and add butter, spreading around to cover entire surface of skillet.

6. Add the egg mixture to the skillet.

7. When the edges of the egg mixture begin to set, use a heatproof silicone spatula to move the egg up away from the edge.

8. After about 2 more minutes, lift the skillet away from the heat and with your other hand, run the spatula around the edge of the eggs in the skillet.

9   Then gently run the spatula underneath the omelet lifting it away from the skillet. As you lift the eggs up away from the skillet, turn the pan slightly to allow the liquid eggs to run underneath the already cooked egg portion of the omelet. Perform this motion so that as much of the liquid egg runs off the top of the omelet as you can.

10 Remove spatula, allowing the eggs to fall back into the skillet and place back on heat.

11a To flip: After 1 more minute of cooking on the heat, the eggs should look mostly set. Hold the skillet in your hand away from the heat and in one motion move your hand (and the skillet) toward your body and flick your wrist up (so that your hand moves upward about 2 inches) in order to flip the omelet. If the omelet did not flip entirely, use the spatula so that the top, uncooked side is entirely facing down on the heat.

11b Or not to flip: If you don't want to flip your omelet, simply move on to the next step. The only difference is that you will have to wait an extra minute or two for your eggs to set. If the eggs are still very runny after you add the vegetables and cheese, cover with a lid or another skillet for 2 minutes.

12 Add vegetables and shredded cheese, allow to melt for 1 minute.

13 Slide the omelet from the skillet onto a plate and, when half of the omelet has slid on to the plate, use the edge of the skillet to fold the second half on top making a half moon shape and sealing the cheese inside.

14 Pour the salsa over the top and serve immediately.

Turkey Chili

Max: Contrary to popular thought, turkey exists as more than sliced deli-style and whole bird Thanksgiving-style. Here we use turkey as opposed to ground beef or chicken because it's healthier and still has great flavor. (I guess you could make it with chicken or beef if you want...but that would really offend us because we spent a lot of time writing this book so...I mean, keep that in mind).

Heat

 Main Course

 Serves 6–8

 Prep time 15 minutes/Total time 45 minutes

4 tablespoons **blended oil**, page 47
24 ounces **ground turkey** meat
1 ½ cups diced **onion**, ½-inch pieces
1 cup diced **green pepper**, ½-inch pieces
2 large cloves of **garlic**, minced
1 cup **dark beer** (optional)
1 can (24 ounce) crushed **tomatoes**
1 cup **chicken broth**
½ teaspoon **cayenne pepper**
1 can (12 ounce) **kidney beans**
3 tablespoons **chili powder**
1 teaspoon **cumin**
salt and **pepper** to taste

1 In a large pot, heat 2 tablespoons of oil over medium heat. Brown the turkey meat, and then set aside.

2 Pour out any excess liquid from the pot, and heat remaining oil. Add the onions and green pepper and sauté on medium-high for about 10 minutes, until onion is translucent and very lightly browned.

3 Add garlic and cook for 1 minute more.

4 Pour in the beer if using and simmer on high until most of the liquid is cooked off and it looks syrupy.

5 Add crushed tomatoes, chicken broth, and cooked turkey back to the pot. Simmer on low for 30 minutes.

6 Add cayenne pepper, kidney beans, chili powder, and cumin and simmer for 5 more minutes.

7 Add salt and pepper to taste.

Eli: In Los Angeles where I live, people are into eating healthy (or at least everyone says they are). This sandwich calls for some veggies that you may not buy on a regular basis but I guarantee that the flavors combine to make a unique and tasty sandwich. And it sounds and looks healthy too! Hey — who said image wasn't important?

The Grilled "Incre-ah-dable Veg-ah-table" Sandwich

Heat

Main Course

Serves 1

Total time 15 minutes

1 small **eggplant**, sliced to ¼-inch
1 small **zucchini**, sliced to ¼-inch
1 **tomato**, sliced to ¼-inch
1 **cucumber**, sliced to ¼-inch
2 tablespoon **blended oil**, page 47
1 **onion roll** or 2 slices **Rye bread**
2 ounces **cream cheese**
¼ cup **sprouts**
5 large pieces of **spinach**
salt and **pepper** to taste
pickle spear (optional)

1   Sprinkle the eggplant and zucchini lightly with salt and pepper. In a frying pan, heat the oil over medium-high heat. Add 5 slices each of eggplant and zucchini, taking care not to crowd the pan (See Kitchen Tip: Sauté, page 52). Cook 1–2 minutes each side or until golden brown on both sides.

2   Toast the roll or bread, and then spread the cream cheese on it.

3   Place the zucchini and eggplant slices over the cream cheese.

4   Layer one layer of cucumber slices and one layer of tomato slices, and top with sprouts and spinach.

5   Sprinkle salt and pepper to taste. Close it up and serve immediately with a pickle spear.

71

Vegetarian

Delig

Words like tofu, meatless, vegetables and vegetarian can induce as much dread as a stats class or cleaning the grill at the fast food burger joint you worked at that one summer—but it doesn't need to be that way. If you are here reading this then you are more daring and experimental with your food choices than many other people. If you hadn't heard, things like vegetables and fruits fall under the health umbrella. Remember the food pyramid? For a second, let's review. Fruits and veggies — good; ice cream and candy — bad.

You may not believe what you hear about pesticides and genetic modification of products and how they may be harmful. The truth is, the processes are relatively new and no one knows for certain the long-term effects. They could be entirely safe. We aren't here to preach too much about how to alter your diet. As long as you love food and cook it yourself we will be happy. What we do know is that people have been surviving eating fruits and vegetables for thousands of years. We promise if you try these dishes you will be *ecstatically* surprised at how delicious (and healthy) they are.

$ Saver Tip: There are many amazing flavors without meats and seafood. We promise you won't leave the table hungry. Vegetarian doesn't have to mean bite size portions of tofu. In many recipes, by not using meat, (which is the most expensive item in most recipes) you can create a less expensive meal but no less delicious. For those of you meat-eaters, do yourself a favor and don't skip over this chapter. You, too, could learn something new and expand your taste buds.

Tempeh Enchiladas

Vegetarian Delights

 Main Course

 Serves 4

 Total time 45 minutes

8 ounces **tempeh**
3 tablespoons **vegetable oil**
2 cups shredded **Cheddar** or **Monterey Jack cheese**
¼ cup chopped **green onions**
8 corn **tortillas** at room temperature
Enchilada Sauce (recipe below), or use store-bought enchilada sauce
Elote, page 105
Wild Rice Pilaf, page 83

Enchilada Sauce

1 can (8 ounce) crushed or diced **tomatoes**
2 tablespoons **chili powder**
2 teaspoons **oregano**
1 teaspoon **cocoa powder**

1   Preheat oven to 350°F.

2   Cut tempeh into thin strips.

3   Sauté in vegetable oil on medium heat until lightly browned.

4   Distribute tempeh, 1-cup cheese, and green onions in 8 tortillas.

5   Pour half of Enchilada Sauce in bottom of ovenproof dish.

5   Roll each tortilla and place on top of sauce, and then cover with remaining sauce.

6   Sprinkle remaining cheese over the enchiladas and bake for 20 minutes or until cheese is melted.

7   Serve with Elote and Wild Rice Pilaf.

For the Enchilada Sauce

Simmer all ingredients together for 30 minutes.

Sautéed Vegetables

Sautéed veggies cannot be stopped! A no-hassle dish that complements any meat, fish or poultry entrée. Fantastic as a side instead of chips or fries.

This combination of vegetables goes well with any dish, but feel free to change the vegetables according to your taste.

Vegetarian Delights

Side Dish

Serves 2

Total time 15 minutes

2 tablespoons **blended oil** or **vegetable oil**, page 47
1 diced **red pepper**, 1-inch pieces
1 sliced **carrot**, ½-inch pieces
½ diced **red onion**, 1-inch pieces
½ diced head of **broccoli**, 1-inch pieces
salt and **pepper** to taste

1. In a large skillet, heat the blended oil until almost smoking.

2. Add all the vegetables at once.

3. Toss immediately to evenly coat with oil.

4. Sprinkle salt and pepper to taste and toss again.

5. Continue cooking on medium-high, tossing every minute or so, until vegetables are tender, about 4–5 minutes.

Vegetarian Stuffed Peppers

Stuffed peppers are pretty easy going. They can be vegetarian or you can add chicken, beef, sausage or fish. The stuffed peppers recipe below has no cheese or meat but at the bottom we give tips on how to incorporate those if you wish.

Vegetarian Delights

Main Course

Serves 4

Total time 45 minutes

4 large **green peppers** (make sure the peppers can stand on their own on a flat surface and not fall)

¼ cup extra virgin **olive oil**

½ diced **red onion**, ¼-inch pieces

½ diced **red pepper**, ¼-inch pieces

1 diced **tomato**, ½-inch pieces

2 cloves of **garlic**, minced

1 recipe of **Wild Rice Pilaf**, page 83

1 tablespoon **basil**

1 tablespoon **oregano**

¼ cup **Italian breadcrumbs** or **Homemade Breadcrumbs**, page 128

salt and **pepper**

1 Preheat oven to 350°F.

2 Cut the tops of the peppers about 1-inch below the stem. Clean out the inside of the peppers removing all seeds. Save tops and set aside.

3 In a skillet, heat the olive oil on medium heat until it shimmers.

4 Add the red onion and red pepper and cook 5 minutes stirring often to avoid burning.

5 Add the tomato and the garlic. Turn heat down to low and cook for 2 more minutes.

6 Mix in the rice, basil, oregano, and breadcrumbs.

7 Take the green peppers and place in the microwave on high for 30 seconds.

8 Place the green peppers on an oven safe cooking dish and fill them with the rice and vegetable mixture. Place the tops back on the pepper.

9 Bake in foil-covered ovenproof dish with 1-inch of water until peppers soften, about 20–30 minutes.

Variation

Cheese: After cooking, sprinkle shredded cheese on top before serving.

Meat: Use about ¼-pound of ground beef. Cook the meat fully in a separate skillet with 1 tablespoon vegetable oil and some salt and pepper. Add cooked meat to the vegetable mixture, and then proceed with the next step.

Veggie Burger Crumbles: Thaw and break apart with your hands, then stir-fry before adding to mixture.

TVP: Textured Vegetable Protein, a vegetarian's friend. TVP is a soy-based substitute for ground beef. Reconstitute according to directions on package, and stir-fry with some onions and garlic before adding to mixture.

Eggplant Parmesan

Even if you have preconceived notions about eggplants (like many people do) give eggplant another chance with this dish that is sure to make you change your mind.

Vegetarian Delights

 Main Course

 Serves 6–8

 Prep time 30 minutes/Total time 1 hour

2 large **eggplants**, sliced to ½-inch (enough for 2 layers in a 9 x 13 baking dish)

kosher salt

½ cup **flour**

3 **eggs**, beaten

1–1 ½ cups **Italian flavored breadcrumbs**, or **Homemade Breadcrumbs**, page 128

3 tablespoons **blended oil**, page 47

1 jar (24 ounce) **marinara sauce**, or **Homemade Marinara Sauce**, page 145

½ cup grated **Parmesan cheese**

½ pound shredded **mozzarella cheese**

1. Lightly toss the sliced eggplant with kosher salt and let sit in a colander for 30 minutes. Drain and press the eggplant with paper towel to dry.

2. Preheat oven to 425°F.

3. Brush a cookie sheet with oil.

4. Coat eggplant slices in flour and shake off excess flour. Dip flour-coated eggplant slices in egg, then in breadcrumbs, shaking off excess breadcrumbs.

5. Place in a single layer on the baking sheet. Bake until golden brown, about 5–7 minutes on each side. Remove from oven and reduce heat to 375°F.

6. Spread one-third of the Marinara Sauce on the bottom of a 9 x 13 baking dish.

7. Layer eggplant slices evenly over the Marinara Sauce.

8   Sprinkle with half the Parmesan cheese.

9   Pour half the remaining Marinara Sauce over the eggplant slices. Layer remaining eggplant slices if you have any.

10 Cover with remaining sauce, mozzarella and Parmesan cheese.

11 Bake in oven until golden brown and bubbly, about 30–40 minutes.

Sophisticated Crowd-Pleaser Tip: Another way to serve this dish, especially good if you're cooking for a smaller crowd: get the eggplant slices nice and crispy, then stack them with a slice of tomato, fresh mozzarella, and a fresh basil leaf in a small tower (see Salmon and Goat Cheese Napoleon, page 132, for another stacked dish). Spread a few tablespoons of marinara sauce on the plate and you've got a fancy restaurant version of Eggplant Parmesan.

Grilled Eggplant and Arugula

Max: This dish combines some of my favorite flavors: eggplant, Parmesan, arugula, and balsamic vinegar. Try it out for some light vegetarian fare.

Vegetarian Delights

 Main Course

 Serves 4

 Total time 35 minutes

1 large **eggplant**
salt and **pepper**
¼ cup extra virgin **olive oil**
½ cup grated **Parmesan cheese**
1 package (10 ounce) **baby arugula**
balsamic vinegar

1   Preheat oven to 400°F.

2   Slice eggplant to ½-inch.

3   Sprinkle each slice lightly with salt and pepper.

4   Brush generously with extra virgin olive oil.

5   Grill each slice until softened, about 2–4 minutes per side, depending on your grill temperature.

6   Remove from grill and arrange on a baking sheet.

7   Sprinkle Parmesan cheese over each slice and bake until cheese is lightly browned, about 5–6 minutes.

8   Remove from oven, and place a small amount of arugula over each slice.

9   Drizzle lightly with balsamic vinegar and olive oil and serve.

Linguine and Herbs

Any restaurant can throw together their interpretation of linguine and herbs, but this ain't just any herbs here. We mean fresh, off the plant herbs.

This dish is great to eat in a pinch by itself, but if you've got some more time you can use it to accompany other dishes, like Breaded Tilapia with Herb Butter, page 118, and Pan-Seared Steak, page 117.

Vegetarian Delights

Main Course

Serves 4

Total time 20 minutes

½ pound dry **linguine**
3 tablespoons **Herb Butter**, page 126
salt and **pepper**

1 Cook pasta according to directions on the box.

2 Drain pasta, toss with Herb Butter and salt and pepper to taste.

Pasta Primavera

The trick to this recipe is not letting the vegetables overcook. It's supposed to be a light dish with the focus on the veggies, so as long as you don't turn them into a mushy mess you'll end up with a delicious meal.

Vegetarian Delights

 Main Course

 Serves 2–4

 Total time 30 minutes

½ pound dry **angel hair** or **spaghetti**

4 tablespoons extra virgin **olive oil**

½ cup diced **onion**, ½-inch pieces

¼ cup diced **carrots**, ½-inch pieces

1 clove **garlic**, thinly sliced

½ cup chopped **broccoli**

¼ cup **peas** (if frozen, rinse to remove ice chunks)

½ cup diced **zucchini**, ¾-inch pieces

¼ cup **cherry tomatoes**, halved

salt and **pepper** to taste

¼ cup **Parmesan cheese**

1 Cook pasta according to directions on the box. Drain pasta, toss with half the olive oil and set aside.

2 Heat remaining oil in nonstick frying pan on medium-high until hot.

3 Add onions and carrots and sauté for 4 minutes.

4 Add garlic and sauté for 1 minute.

5 Add broccoli, peas, and zucchini; sauté 1–2 more minutes.

6 Reduce heat to low and add tomatoes.

7 Toss with pasta and add salt and pepper to taste.

8 Serve with Parmesan cheese.

Wild Rice Pilaf

We live dangerously, which is why this dish isn't called "boring white rice pilaf." We don't have a problem with our friend "white rice" except that whenever we go out he always gets tired at 10 and makes us drop him off. On the other hand "wild rice" likes to party all night long!

Vegetarian Delights

Side Dish

Serves 2

Prep time 10 minutes/Total time 55 minutes

2 tablespoons **butter**
¼ cup diced **onion**, ¼-inch pieces
1 cup **brown rice**
¼ cup **wild rice**
2 ¾ cups **water**
¼ cup diced **carrot**, ¼-inch pieces

1   Melt the butter in a medium pot. Sauté onion in butter until softened slightly, about 4–5 minutes.

2   Add rice and cook for another 3–4 minutes, stirring constantly.

3   Add water and bring to a boil.

4   Reduce heat, cover, and simmer on low until most of the water is absorbed, about 30 minutes. Add carrots and continue cooking until all water is absorbed.

5   Remove from heat, let stand for 10 minutes. Fluff with fork and serve.

In this recipe the creaminess of the risotto goes so well with the mushrooms' rich, meaty flavor. With Parmesan cheese, it's a classic dish that works as a meal or as a complement to fish, poultry or meat. Remember to use Arborio rice!

Mushroom and Herb Risotto

Vegetarian Delights

Main Course / Side Dish

Serves 2–4

Total time 45 minutes

2 tablespoons butter or extra virgin **olive oil**

1 cup diced **onion**, ¼-inch pieces

1 clove **garlic**, minced

6 ounces **button mushrooms**, sliced into medium sized pieces

1 ounce **dried porcini mushroom**s, re-hydrated (optional), page 59

2 cups **Arborio rice**

1 cup **white wine**

4–6 cups **vegetable stock**, more as needed

2 teaspoons finely chopped fresh **sage**

2 teaspoons finely chopped fresh **rosemary**

2 teaspoons finely chopped fresh **parsley**

2 teaspoons finely chopped fresh **oregano**

½ cup **Parmesan cheese** grated

salt and **pepper** to taste

1 In a heavy soup pot, heat the butter or oil. Add the onions and cook until soft, about 6–7 minutes. Add garlic and cook for 1–2 more minutes.

2 Add the mushrooms and cook for 3–4 more minutes.

3 Add the rice and cook until edges of rice became translucent, taking care not to burn the rice, about 3–4 minutes.

4 Add the wine and cook until most of the liquid has cooked away.

5 Add enough stock so that the rice is barely covered. When the liquid begins to cook down, add ½-cup more stock, stirring constantly.

6 Repeat this process until half the liquid is gone.

7 Add the herbs and continue adding liquid until rice is tender, stirring constantly.

8 Add half the Parmesan cheese and mix well; salt and pepper to taste.

9 Serve in bowls garnished with herbs and remaining cheese.

Mac and Cheese

This recipe is so much better than a box version it's ridiculous. You won't believe it until you make it. And you have to make it. Honestly, if you don't, you will be missing out. Huge.

Vegetarian Delights

 Main Course

 Serves 4

 Prep time 20 minutes/Total time 1 hour

½ pound dry **elbow macaroni**
2 tablespoons extra virgin **olive oil**
2 tablespoons **butter**
1 small **onion**, medium dice
2 teaspoons **garlic**, minced
2 tablespoons **flour**
1 ¾ cup **milk**
6 ounces **Gruyère cheese**, shredded
6 ounces Extra Sharp **Cheddar cheese**, shredded
2 ounces **Parmesan cheese**, shredded
salt and **pepper** to taste

1. Preheat oven to 350°F.

2. Cook pasta according to directions on the box, minus 3 minutes. The pasta should be more firm than usual. Drain pasta, toss with olive oil and set aside.

3. In a medium saucepan, melt the butter. Add the onion and sauté on medium heat until translucent, about 4–5 minutes.

4. Add the garlic and sauté for 1 more minute.

5. Add the flour and mix well. Cook, stirring constantly with a wooden spoon, for 2–3 minutes.

6. Add the milk slowly, whisking well (whisk, page 12).

7. When all the milk is added, add all but 1-cup of the cheeses.

8. Toss the pasta with the cheese sauce and season with salt and pepper to taste.

9. Pour into a 9-inch square ovenproof dish. Sprinkle remaining cheese over the top.

10. Bake until bubbly and brown, approximately 30–40 minutes.

 $ Saver Tip: We realize your wallet may be a little tight and 3 cheeses may be pricey. Feel free to switch the Gruyere cheese with Swiss or just use Cheddar — or even some Pepper Jack. As long as the total amount of cheese remains the same it will turn out great.

Pesto Pasta

Max: Fresh pesto is a vegetarian dish that non-vegetarians will love. Make a big batch and freeze single servings in plastic bags to use whenever you want. If you don't have a food processor, you can make this in the blender, but you will have to stir things around with a spoon from time to time to make sure everything blends (remember to turn off the blender first, of course).

Eli: I picture you serving this pasta dish piping hot to a table full of friends over for dinner. All of you sit around laughing, sharing stories, eating this delicious pasta and making memories sure to be displayed within hours on a photo-sharing, social networking website. Then the next day, you go to the fridge, sit down on the couch to watch re-runs and eat the leftovers cold. And it's delicious both ways.

Vegetarian Delights

Main Course

Serves 2–4

Total time 30 minutes

¼ cup **pine nuts**

1–2 cloves **garlic**

1 cup fresh **basil** leaves, tightly packed

¼ cup extra virgin **olive oil**

½ cup grated **Parmesan cheese**, plus more for topping

salt to taste

½ pound dry **penne** or **spaghetti**

2 tablespoons **unsalted butter**

1. Toast the pine nuts by placing them on a cookie sheet in a preheated 350°F oven for a few minutes, until light golden brown.

2. Cut the garlic into a few pieces, and then place it and the basil and garlic in the food processor. Blend, adding the olive oil slowly with the processor running.

3. Add the Parmesan and pine nuts and process again.

4. Add salt to taste.

5. Cook pasta according to directions on the box. Drain pasta, and then toss with butter and desired amount of pesto. Top with more Parmesan cheese and serve immediately.

Variations

Toasted Walnut: Replace some or all of the pine nuts with toasted walnuts.

Arugula: Replace some or all of the basil with baby arugula.

Sun-dried Tomato: Add a few sun-dried tomatoes with the basil in Step 2.

Sesame Peanut Noodles

Max: This dish has developed a trendy following as of late, but my version was first. Okay, maybe not the very first, but it's got a serious chance in a Sesame Peanut Noodle battle. It is best served cold with fresh chopped green onions sprinkled over the top. Try adding a chopped chicken breast or salmon fillet.

Vegetarian Delights

Main Course

Serves 2–4

Total time 20 minutes

½ pound dry **spaghetti**

3 tablespoons toasted **sesame oil**

¼ cup crunchy **peanut butter**

¼ cup **soy sauce**

1 tablespoon **seasoned rice vinegar**

1 teaspoon **chili sauce**

3 tablespoons **water**

1 teaspoon **brown sugar**

1 small clove minced **garlic**

1 tablespoon minced **ginger**

1 **carrot**, shredded

3 **green onions**, thinly sliced

1 **cucumber**, medium dice

1 tablespoon **sesame seeds**

1 Cook spaghetti according to directions on the box. Drain and rinse pasta, then toss with 2 tablespoons sesame oil.

2 Combine peanut butter, soy sauce, seasoned rice vinegar, chili sauce, water, brown sugar, garlic, ginger, and remaining tablespoon of sesame oil in a mixing bowl.

3 Toss the pasta with the peanut sauce mixture, ½ the carrot, ½ the green onion, and cucumber.

4 Transfer to a serving dish and garnish with sesame seeds, remaining carrot, and remaining green onion.

Szechwan Stir-fry with Tofu and Basmati Rice

The trick to this dish is to have no fear. Everyone has their own personal style so if you find yourself wanting to add or subtract certain ingredients, make it spicier or add barbeque sauce, by all means go right ahead. Stir-frying is more about quickly cooking vegetables and meat over high heat (preferably in a wok) than the actual ingredients used, so go ahead and experiment.

Vegetarian Delights

 Main Course

 Serves 4

 Total time 30 minutes

1 pound sliced firm **tofu**, ¾-inch thick pieces
4 tablespoons **canola** or **vegetable oil**
½ cup diced **onion**, ¾-inch pieces
1 tablespoon minced **garlic**
1 tablespoon minced **ginger**
½ cup sliced peeled **carrot**, ¼-inch thick slices
½ cup diced **red pepper**, ¾-inch pieces
½ cup chopped **broccoli**
Basmati Rice, recipe following

Sauce

1 tablespoon **Szechwan** or **Hot Bean Paste***
1 tablespoon **soy sauce**
1 tablespoon Sriracha or other **chili sauce***
available at Asian markets or in Asian section of grocery stores.

1   Make Sauce by mixing bean paste, soy sauce, and chili paste. Set aside.

2   Place ¾-inch sliced tofu on several layers of paper towel, add additional paper towel on top, and place a heavy pot or pan over it all to press out the moisture (anything to add weight works). This step is important, as it will ensure good even frying of the tofu. Press for 10 minutes then cut the slices into ¾-inch cubes.

3   Heat 2 tablespoons oil until very hot in a wok or frying pan. Add the tofu and toss or stir rapidly until it is lightly browned on all sides, about 5 minutes. Add 2 tablespoons soy sauce and cook for 1 more minute, then remove tofu and set aside.

4   Wipe out the wok or frying pan with a paper towel or kitchen towel.

5   Heat 2 tablespoons oil until very hot. Add onion, garlic, and ginger, and cook for 2 minutes. Reduce heat or remove from heat if necessary to prevent burning.

6   Add the rest of the vegetables and sauté until just tender, 3–4 minutes.

7   Add Sauce and reserved tofu, toss well.

8   Serve with Basmati Rice.

Basmati rice has an amazing flavor and aroma. The key to making great white rice is, first, use the right amount of water; second, cook on a very low heat; and third, let the rice stand for 10 minutes before you eat it.

Basmati Rice

1 cup **Basmati rice**

2 cups **water**

Basmati Rice

1. Place the water and rice in a medium saucepan and bring to a boil.

2. Immediately reduce to a low simmer and continue cooking until all liquid is absorbed into the rice, about 10–15 minutes.

3. Let stand 10 minutes before serving.

Note on rice cooking: While the 2:1 ratio of water to rice works well for 1 cup of rice, if you are going to be making more than 1 cup you will need to decrease the total amount of water slightly.

Grilli

All grills are not made equal. Coal and gas grills will cook differently and the food may taste differently too. Also, no coal stack will heat the same way twice. Once you actually get down to it, it will just be you, the grill and your food, so welcome to the jungle. This jungle isn't fun and games. A huge heat source outside can be very dangerous. In the cooking business we call this a potential...(get ready for it) "recipe for disaster!" But in all seriousness, great grilling can turn a meal into a feast and a gathering into an event. Here are a few tips to help keep you and those around you safe, full and having fun.

1. Fire Bad. Safety Good. Man Dumb.

Coals don't need to look red or be flaming to be extremely hot. I know you are curious but don't touch them with your hands. You are better than that. Stay close by while grilling and always keep an eye out for people coming too close to the grill. If there is alcohol around or it is nighttime, pay extra attention that the grill is off to the side so that people not paying attention don't stumble upon a dark black metal box filled with fire. The last thing you want is to have to drive someone to the ER with one hand while you eat a steak with the other. It's not the best way to eat and speaking from experience you will spill BBQ sauce everywhere. Don't have the grill on dry grass or something that can catch fire easily. Keeping water or sand nearby to put out a fire is another great idea that we came up with all by ourselves.

2. Dad Wisdom Says: 'The Longer It Takes, The Better It Tastes!'

Grilling is not a fast process. It will take a while to get the coals hot. Even a gas grill needs to heat up for a few minutes. Then the meat will take a bit to cook, too. Grilling is an experience. Get a cold beverage and savor the fresh air outside (please tell me you aren't inside!). The key to amazing grilling is that the meat cooks while getting flavor from the fire, the marinade and the juices in the meat. If you cook the food too quickly, over a charcoal fire before it's ready, your meat will definitely burn before it cooks. Of course if you cook the food too slowly, it will be gray, dry, and tough on the inside. If you like that flavor combo, save yourself time and go try that new 'fire roasted cardboard flavor gum' (hopefully that didn't sound appealing or we might as well give up now).

3. Be Like Your Favorite Rapper and Buy a Grill You'll Love

When buying a grill, find what works best for you. Some people like gas grills while others prefer coals. Some prefer a huge multi-level grill that will do your taxes while some go with a simple single flat grill with a dome top (the classic). Coal chimneys are an easy way to get the fire started and can be bought at your local hardware, home goods or cooking store. They work better than trying to build a pyramid of coals, letting lighter fluid soak in and then trying to keep the heat on task. To avoid any culinary disputes, we publicly declare we love BOTH gas and charcoal grills equally.

4. You Ain't Too Cool For School, So Use a Tool

Using your hands to move food on the grill is gross, and can be painful as well. You can burn yourself and you shouldn't touch raw meat if you're going to be touching cooked meat right after. Some useful grill tools are metal spatulas, long grill tongs, large meat fork, meat thermometer and a couple of pans for food when completed. You can get all that in a grill tool set at your local hardware store. A small side table to hold all your tools, your beverage of choice and some "tune-age" also help make the cooking experience all that more enjoyable.

The grill is the perfect cooking tool for so many situations.
Pick your favorite!

1: People coming over for an outdoor birthday party (superheroes themed?? Ummm obviously!)

2: A summer day when you feel like cooking outside. More lemonade please!

3: Flag Day, President's Day, Take Your Pet to Work Day, Laundry Day, Monday.

4: Celebrate Global Warming existing OR not existing! Win-Win!

5: Put off those pesky bills by starting the fire with them! Then cook stuff on the fire!

6: Hot Temp. + Outside + Sprinkler (or kiddie pool) + Grill = Let's drink beers all day long!!!! (Must be 21 for this option.)

Use the grill as much as you can when weather allows you to. If you are like many people, you are living in a climate where you will be forced indoors for months due to cold. (If not, you are one lucky soul!) So soak up the sun and fire up that grill!

Meat On The Grill — Using a Thermometer

It's easy to overcook red meat. Everyone has their own preference, but I prefer steaks medium-rare and burgers medium or medium-rare. You should know that if you like your red meat red, then it will be a much lower temperature than the 'recommended' cooked temperature of 145°F. If you like your burgers done all the way through, then 165°F is the way to go. When in doubt, especially with a burger, you can always take a knife and peek on the inside. Keep in mind, though, that meat continues to cook for about 5 minutes after you remove it from heat, so it will be slightly more done than when you check it on the grill.

Grilling Fish

Grilling Fish can be tricky, since the fish has a tendency to fall apart (unlike red meat). The trick is to allow the grill to get very very hot (leave the grill covered for this). Make sure the grill surface itself is very clean, and then wipe with some vegetable oil. Place your fish down on the grill, and don't move it until it is ready to turn (3–5 minutes, depending on the thickness of the fish). Then, using a spatula carefully flip the fish and cook until just done (should be tender, not firm). Good luck!

Grill Thermometer

A meat thermometer is a key ingredient, especially for items that really should not be consumed undercooked, like poultry. An instant-read, electric thermometer is your best bet here. If you're using the simpler analog version, you will have to make sure your thermometer is calibrated and accurate. To do this, submerge in ice water and ensure that the temperature reads 32 degrees Fahrenheit. If not, adjust until temperature is accurate.

To use the thermometer, stick into the thickest portion of the meat, wait 5 seconds until temperature is steady, and read.

RED MEAT

Rare 120–125°F
red center, pink outer ring, cooked
outside only

Med. Rare 130–135°F
pink center, outer ring is more cooked,
cooked outside

Med. 140–145°F
light pink center, outer portion is
browned and cooked

Med. Well 150–155°F
no pink color

Well 160°F
entire steak is cooked throughout with
no pink, very dark exterior cooked

Ground beef 165°F

POULTRY

165°F cook until juice is clear

SEAFOOD

Tuna, swordfish, marlin 125°F
cook until medium rare (fish should
be darker colored in center, basically
not cooked)

Ari's Asian BBQ Marinade/Glaze

Max: My roommate Ari made this marinade for a barbeque we had, and it was a huge hit. For the marinade to work its magic, try to get as much of your chicken or tofu as possible submerged under the liquid, and turn it every couple hours. You can use the marinade as a basting liquid once you are grilling—just make sure to throw it away once the meat comes off the grill because raw chicken juice is not healthy.

Grilling

 Marinade

 Yields approximately 1 ½ cups

 Total time 15 minutes

2/3 cup **Korean BBQ Sauce**

¼ cup **soy sauce**

¼ cup **mirin** (sweet rice wine)

2 tablespoons **rice vinegar**

1 tablespoon **sesame oil**

1 tablespoon **Sriracha Chili Sauce** (available at Asian markets and many supermarkets)

2 large cloves **garlic**, finely minced

1 inch **ginger** root, finely minced

Mix all ingredients together. For chicken, marinate 6 hours to overnight. For tofu, marinade for 48 hours.

Asian Chicken Skewers

Grilling

Main Course

Yields 8 skewers

Total time 40 minutes

2 diced **chicken breasts**, 1-inch pieces
    marinated in Ari's Asian BBQ Marinade,
    page 98
1 diced **red pepper**, 1-inch pieces
1 diced **red onion**, 1-inch pieces
4 ounces fresh **button mushrooms**
1 diced **zucchini**, 1-inch pieces
8 wooden **skewers**

Asian may not be the first flavor you think of when the grill gets going but it's a change of pace from the "same old same old." It's one of our favorite ways to season meat for the grill.

1 Place the diced chicken and vegetables on the skewers.

2 Grill on medium-high for 10 minutes, turning every 2–3 minutes, or until chicken is cooked through.

3 Serve immediately.

Awesome Meat Marinade

Eli: This distinctive marinade goes really well with red meat. It was invented in the Franklin House kitchen in Los Feliz. Allow the meat to marinate for minimum 2 hours but 8 hours is optimal. This is enough marinade to cover 2 steaks.

Grilling

 Marinade

 Yields 2 cups of marinade

 Total time 15 minutes

½ cup **white wine**

½ cup **red wine**

3 large cloves **garlic**, minced

1 teaspoon **distilled white vinegar**

6 small diced **pearl onions**, ½-inch pieces

3 tablespoons **Worcestershire sauce**

1 tablespoon minced **ginger**

1 cup **beef broth**

1 Combine all ingredients.

2 Cover meat with marinade for up to 8 hours and refrigerate, turning every few hours.

Citrus-Chili Glaze

This southwest glaze is perfect for chicken, salmon and shrimp. This stuff is deliciously potent so keep some close to the grill to brush onto your food periodically.

Grilling

Glaze

Yields about 2–3 cups

Prep time 10 minutes / Total time 1 hour

4 cups **orange juice**

1 tablespoon **lemon juice**

½ cup **white wine** (optional)

2 teaspoons **cayenne pepper**

½ teaspoon **ground ginger**

½ teaspoon **Dijon mustard**

1   Mix all ingredients together in large saucepot.

2   Simmer on medium until liquid becomes slightly syrupy and lightly coats the back of a spoon, about 45–50 minutes.

3   Remove from heat.

4   Brush glaze on chicken breasts, tofu, salmon, or shrimp while grilling.

Brining

Brine is just a word for saltwater, and soaking meats in saltwater is called brining. The meat has less salt and less water than the saltwater solution, so when you brine meat, the salty water rushes over to the meat — just like in Chemistry 101. All this adds up to juicy, flavorful meat. Try it with meats that tend to dry out, like chicken and pork chops.

A good ratio to go by is 1 cup of Kosher salt to 1 gallon of water. You should brine the meat for about an hour per pound. Make sure the meat is submerged underneath the water.

A good trick to getting all the meat submerged using minimal space is to pack it tightly in zip-close bags, then pour your brine over it. Close the bag and store it in a baking dish to avoid spills in the refrigerator.

BBQ Chicken

BBQ chicken is not as easy as you think. Putting the sauce on too early does not allow the chicken to properly cook and you end up burning off a lot of the great flavor from the sauce. Brining the chicken (see how to do this by reading adjacent page), if you have time, will increase the moisture and flavor of the chicken. These instructions will give you the best, most moist and flavorful chicken every time. It's a sweet science and practice makes perfect.

An alternative way to make this recipe (pictured here) is to use a whole cut-up chicken. Make sure to take the temperature of each piece separately since dark meat and light meat cook at different rates.

Grilling

Main Course

Serves 4

Total time 20 minutes

8 cups **water**
½ cup **salt**
4 **chicken breasts** on the bone
salt and **pepper** to taste
2 cups store-bought **BBQ sauce**

1   Mix salt with water and submerge chicken in the saltwater (see instructions at left for brining). Place in refrigerator.

2   Remove chicken from saltwater and pat dry with paper towels.

3   Sprinkle lightly with salt and pepper.

4   Grill on high for 3–4 minutes, until chicken skin appears medium brown and crispy.

5   Reduce heat to low and cook for 5 minutes.

6   Brush generously with BBQ sauce and cook for 5 more minutes.

7   Repeat step 6.

Grilled Asparagus

Max: The art of grilling asparagus is something I perfected while working at a restaurant in Ann Arbor. Among the things I learned:

1 – The asparagus is the main flavor and it doesn't need much else, just some salt and pepper.

2 – Don't overcook the asparagus! Only cook the asparagus for a few minutes, it's better undercooked, and it will continue cooking for a minute after you remove it from the heat.

3 – If you're going to let it cool before you serve it, lay it out in a single layer so it doesn't continue cooking in its own steam.

Follow these simple steps and you will be amazed at the result!

Grilling

 Side Dish

 Serves 4

 Total time 10 minutes

1 pound **asparagus**
2 tablespoons extra virgin **olive oil**
salt and **pepper** to taste

1   Cut off the bottom inch of the asparagus; this part is tough and won't taste good.

2   Toss with olive oil, salt and pepper.

3   Grill on high for 3–4 minutes, turning every minute or so. They will continue cooking after you remove them from the grill so better to undercook slightly.

Veggie Visual Tip
This graphic shows a piece of asparagus so there won't be any confusion about what is the top and what is the bottom!

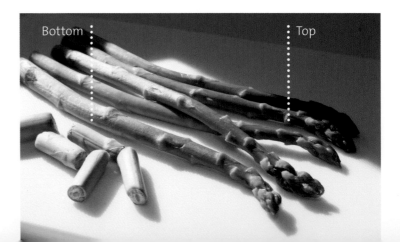

Bottom ⋮   ⋮ Top

Elote
(Mexican Corn on the Cob)

Grilling

Side Dish

Serves 4

Total time 30 minutes

4 ears of **corn**, shucked and cleaned
¼ cup extra virgin **olive oil**
salt and **pepper**
¼ cup **mayonnaise**, **sour cream**, or **butter**
1 tablespoon **lemon juice**
2 tablespoons **hot sauce**
½ cup **Parmesan cheese**, grated

If you've never grilled corn on the cob, you must try this dish. The grill's high cooking temperature brings out different flavors in the corn. The lemon juice and Parmesan add a delicious and unusual contrast to the sweetness of the corn.

1   Lightly brush the corn with olive oil, then sprinkle with salt and pepper.

2   Grill corn until lightly browned on all sides, about 6–7 minutes, rotating every few minutes.

3   Remove corn from heat. When it is cool enough to handle, roll the corn in the mayonnaise, sour cream, or butter, coating evenly.

4   Drizzle the lemon juice and hot sauce over the corn.

5   Sprinkle the Parmesan cheese evenly over the corn and serve.

Hamburger

This recipe is simple but as someone once said, "you're not grilling meatloaf, you're making burgers." Get some good meat and let its flavor come through. The salt and pepper amounts are really a personal preference. Don't taste the raw meat but after doing this a couple times you'll know when you have the right amount of seasoning. As far as seasoning goes, remember, you can always add, but you can't take away.

Grilling

 Main Course

 Serves 4

 Total time 30 minutes

1 pound **ground beef**
salt and **pepper** to taste (½ teaspoon of each recommended)
½ cup minced **onion**
2 cloves of **garlic**, minced
¼ cup extra virgin **olive oil**

1 Mix together the ground beef, salt and pepper, onion, and garlic.

2 Separate the meat into four equal pieces and form each into a round ball. Then flatten each ball out into a patty ½-inch thick.

3 Grill the burger on high 2–3 minutes per side for medium-rare. Add 1 minute per side for medium, and 1 more minute for medium-well.

Variations
Greek Burger
1 Replace ½ pound of ground beef with ½ pound ground lamb.
2 Mix in 1 tablespoon oregano and 3 ounces feta cheese in step 1.

Jamaican Jerk Burger
1 Add 2 teaspoons Jamaican Jerk Seasoning in step 1.
2 Serve with Jamaican Jerk Sauce.

Grilled Portobello Mushrooms

Grilling

Side Dish

Serves 4

Total time 15 minutes

4 **portobello mushrooms**, cleaned gently
under cold water.
¼ cup extra virgin **olive oil**
salt and **pepper** to taste

Portobello mushrooms have a rich meaty consistency that makes them a great substitute for burgers. The wonderful thing about the Portobello mushrooms is they are reasonably priced and are a healthy alternative to meat.

1 Remove stem from mushrooms.

2 Drizzle or brush olive oil evenly on tops and bottoms of mushrooms.

3 Sprinkle mushrooms evenly with salt and pepper.

4 Grill until tender, about 2–3 minutes per side.

Leftovers Tip: Leftover grilled vegetables make a great sandwich the next day. Toast some bread, spread some mayo or Pesto (page 87), add some cheese if you have it and you have a delicious sandwich with almost no extra work.

Grilled Zucchini and Yellow Squash

Grilling

 Side Dish

 Serves 2

 Total time 15 minutes

1 **zucchini**
salt and **pepper** to taste
2 tablespoons extra virgin **olive oil**

Grilled zucchini is delicious! It also looks great when it comes off the grill. We suggest serving it with fresh warm bread as an appetizer.

1 Cut zucchini in half widthwise and then slice lengthwise in ¼-inch slices.

2 Brush with olive oil and sprinkle with salt and pepper.

3 Grill on high, 2 minutes each side.

Eli: Wings rock for a tailgate, BBQ, picnic, dinnertime...anytime. The sauce is really the most vital part of the wings because without a great marinade, the wings are nothin'. I love to make a lot of wings and set some aside to re-heat later on.

Grilling

Main Course

Serves 6

Prep Time 10 minutes/Cook Time 10 minutes

2 pounds **chicken wings**

½ cup **ketchup**

4 **garlic** cloves, peeled

1 cup **teriyaki sauce**

4 tablespoons minced **ginger**

2 tablespoons **unsalted butter**

1 tablespoon **honey**

4 ounces (½ stick) **unsalted butter**

½ cup **ketchup**

¼ cup **vinegar**

4 large cloves **garlic**

2 tablespoons dried **chili flakes**

1 tablespoon **salt**

1 **jalapeño pepper**, minced

Teriyaki Ginger Hot Wings Sauce

1   Combine all ingredients (except wings) in a blender. Blend on high until liquefied.

2   Pour into a 1-gallon size plastic seal bag.

3   Add chicken wings. Allow chicken to marinate overnight.

4   Cook on grill 5 minutes per side.

Hot Hot Hot Sauce

1   Place butter in microwave safe bowl and heat on power level 10 (high) for 20 seconds.

2   Add the remaining ingredients. Pour mixture into blender. Blend on high for 3 minutes or until liquefied.

3   Pour into 1-gallon plastic seal bag.

4   Add chicken wings. Allow chicken to marinate overnight.

5   Cook on grill 5 minutes per side.

Cooking
Impr

to

ess

It just got interesting. You might want to roll up your sleeves now. For some this might be uncharted territory. This chapter takes on a new dynamic. The recipes are going to be increasingly challenging (and you should take some time to make sure the presentation is solid before you serve) but also increasingly rewarding.

There are plenty of people worth impressing. Your friends would love a home cooked meal. So would your roommate. Still not convinced? How about if I told you there was something in it for you. Ok, now you are listening. Nothing impresses the parents more than a nice surprise meal. Now, we understand that dinner out with the parents usually means they are paying at a nicer restaurant than you have been to in months, but try to see that this can be swung to your advantage.

Instead of your parents taking you out and paying, think how wowed they will be when you serve dinner that you made especially for them. They will be caught so off guard that your outlandish demands will be met like you are asking for a stick of gum. Ask them to pay for your spring break trip that they wouldn't even let you go on last week. Bam, you'll be in Mexico before you even know it! Your car needs new brakes? Ask them to throw in that CD changer too! They will be in such a state of shock that you literally can ask them for anything. Shoot for the stars but I would stop short of asking for straight cash. That NEVER works.

In terms of cooking for a date, anyone can buy flowers and go out for sushi. But have you ever made someone a meal from scratch? If there does exist some sort of points scale, cooking a meal from scratch is legitimately off the charts. If your date tells his or her friends about the meal you cooked, their friends will get jealous and say things like "I wish someone would do that for me, you are so lucky." And it's common knowledge that once the friends approve, you can really do no wrong. So it's all time and money very well spent.

This is a great way to prepare chicken in the summer. Get a decent bottle of wine and enjoy it with your meal! We also heard playing board games is cool again so don't be shy — tie that sweater around your neck and go ahead with that post dinner game-athalon of Scrabble, Clue and Twister.

Chicken Breasts with Rosemary, White Wine and Lemon

Cooking to Impress

Main Course

Serves 2

Total time 35 minutes

2 bone-in **chicken breasts**, preferably brined (see page 102 for instructions)

salt and **pepper**

2 tablespoons **vegetable oil**

1 spring fresh **rosemary** or 1 teaspoon dried

1 cup dry **white wine**

⅓ cup **lemon juice**

2 tablespoons **butter**

Linguine and Herbs, page 81 (optional)

Rosemary Potatoes, page 47 (optional)

1   Trim any excess fat and skin from the chicken. Sprinkle chicken with salt and pepper.

2   Heat the oil in a large frying pan and add chicken, skin side down, when hot.

3   Cook for 4–5 minutes, until skin is nicely browned. Turn over and cook for 3 minutes.

4   Add wine and lemon juice and simmer for 5–10 minutes, or until chicken is cooked through.

5   Whisk butter into sauce.

6   Serve with Linguine and Herbs or Roasted Rosemary Potatoes.

Angel Hair with Bacon Cream Sauce and Peas

Cooking to Impress

 Main Course

 Serves 2–4

 Total time 35 minutes

6 strips raw **bacon**

½ pound dry **angel hair pasta**

2 tablespoons extra virgin **olive oil** (more as needed)

¼ cup **onion** or **shallot**, minced

1 clove **garlic**, minced

½ cup frozen **peas**, thawed and rinsed

1 cup **heavy cream**

2 tablespoons grated **Parmesan cheese**

generous freshly **ground pepper**

1 Cut the bacon into 1/8-inch pieces.

2 Cook the bacon in a large skillet over medium heat until crispy.

3 Remove the bacon and set aside on paper towel.

4 Drain all but 2 tablespoons of the bacon fat.

5 Cook pasta according to directions on the box, less 1 minute. Drain pasta, then toss with 2 tablespoons olive oil and set aside.

6 Heat the remaining bacon fat until shimmering.

7 Add the onions and cook over medium heat until soft.

8 Add garlic and peas and cook for 1 minute longer.

9 Add the bacon and cream and cook until simmering.

10 Add pasta, stir to combine, and cook for 1 minute more.

11 Top with Parmesan cheese and freshly ground black pepper.

This is an incredibly rich dish that will keep you warm through the winter. Serve this recipe to 4 people for an appetizer portion or use it for 2 people for a main course.

Sautéed Spinach

Cooking to Impress

 Side Dish

 Serves 2

 Total time 10 minutes

1 tablespoon extra virgin **olive oil**
1 clove **garlic**, minced
salt and **pepper**
1 bag (10 ounce) **baby spinach**

1 Heat oil in a sauté pan on medium heat.

2 When hot, add the garlic and sauté for 1 minute.

3 Add the salt and pepper and spinach and cook until spinach is wilted, stirring regularly, about 3-4 minutes.

Pan Seared Steak

Eli : Anyone who knows me knows that I love steak. When people ask me the three things I would bring to an island, the list always breaks down like this:1-steak, 2-steak, 3-a laptop (what can I say, I love chatting with friends online...). If you don't feel like getting the grill going this is a killer way to cook a steak. Marinating the steak is not necessary, but it will add another layer of flavor if you desire.

Food Lingo: Marbling *refers to fat that is distributed throughout a piece of meat. Unlike the long strips of fat found on the edges that are no good to eat, a steak with lots of marbling will be juicier and more flavorful than one without.*

Cooking to Impress

Main Course

Serves 1

Total time 20 minutes

1 **steak** of your choice (preferably a rib-eye with a good amount of marbling)

¼ cup **teriyaki** or **Worcestershire sauce** (if marinating)

2 tablespoons **blended**, **vegetable**, or **canola oil**, page 47

kosher salt and **pepper**

1   If marinating, cover the raw steak in the teriyaki or Worcestershire sauce. Flip steak to cover all sides. Marinate up to 4 hours if possible but you can cook immediately if desired.

2   Remove steak from the marinade and pat dry with paper towel. Cover all surfaces with olive oil, and sprinkle evenly with salt and pepper.

3   Heat a skillet to high.

4   Add blended oil to the skillet. When it is very hot, add the steak.

5   Cook 3–4 minutes on each side for medium-rare, depending on thickness of steak.

6   Let steak rest for 5 minutes before eating.

Tasty Tip: When seasoning steak, kosher salt works best. You can pick up the salt between your fingers and sprinkle it evenly over the meat without it becoming too salty, unlike regular iodized salt, which has much finer crystals.

Breaded Tilapia with Herb Butter

Cooking to Impress

 Main Course

 Serves 2

 Total time 30 minutes

2 **eggs**
2 (6-ounce) **tilapia** filets
1 cup **Italian breadcrumbs** or **Homemade Breadcrumbs**, page 128
2 tablespoons **Herb Butter**, page 126
1 teaspoon **mayonnaise**
1 tablespoons **lemon juice**
3 tablespoons **blended oil**, page 47
Wild Rice Pilaf, page 83

Tilapia is a very common saltwater fish with a mild taste. It readily accepts the flavors that you cook it in creating a perfectly seasoned dish. It grills, bakes and broils brilliantly.

1 Lightly beat the eggs.

2 Bread the tilapia by dipping in egg, then coating well with breadcrumbs.

3 Melt the Herb Butter in a small skillet or microwave. Let cool slightly, then mix in mayonnaise and lemon juice and set aside. The lemon juice may not dissolve into the butter and that's ok.

4 Heat a nonstick skillet to medium-high and then add oil. Gently place the tilapia in the pan and fry until golden brown on one side, about 2–3 minutes. Carefully flip and cook on the other side until golden brown and cooked through.

5 Serve with the lemon-herb butter-mayonnaise mix and Wild Rice Pilaf.

Spicy Rainbow Trout

Cooking to Impress

Main Course

Serves 2

Total time 25 minutes

1 teaspoon **salt**

1 teaspoon **pepper**

1 tablespoon **paprika**

1 teaspoon **cayenne pepper**

1 teaspoon **oregano**

½ cup **flour**

2 (6-ounce) **rainbow trout** filets

2 tablespoons **blended oil**, page 47

The more popular salmon and tuna often overshadow rainbow trout, but don't overlook rainbow trout's tender and mild flavor. If you can't find fresh trout, feel free to use this recipe with any other firm-fleshed fish.

1. Mix all spices together.

2. Divide spice mix in half. Mix one half with the flour, and set the other half aside.

3. Evenly sprinkle the flesh side of the fish with the spice mix.

4. Evenly coat the fish with the spiced flour. Shake off excess flour.

5. Heat skillet on high with blended oil. When very hot, gently place the fish flesh side down in the pan.

6. Cook for 2–3 minutes, and then gently flip. Reduce heat to medium-low and cook for 3–4 more minutes, until fish is cooked through.

Chicken Marsala

Eli: This dish is one of the first dishes I ate in an upscale restaurant that I attempted to duplicate at home. Going off the top of my head proved more difficult than I imagined. So by working through it a few times the result is below. I think you will find it as delicious as it is impressive. The rich flavor makes it the perfect entrée to center a large meal around.

Cooking to Impress

 Main Course

 Serves 2

 Total time here

2 large boneless **chicken breasts**

salt and **pepper**

½ cup all-purpose **flour**

2 tablespoons **blended oil**, page 47, or extra virgin **olive oil**

½ small diced **onion**, ¼-inch pieces

1 clove **garlic**, minced

8 ounces **button** or **crimini/baby portabello mushrooms**, thinly sliced

pinch of **salt**

½ cup **Marsala**

½ cup **chicken stock**

1 teaspoon **cornstarch**

2 teaspoons **water**

8 ounces **egg noodles**

2 tablespoons **butter**

1. Lightly season the chicken by sprinkling with salt and pepper, and coat in flour.

2. Heat the oil over medium-high heat in a large skillet. Shake off excess flour from the chicken and place in skillet. Cook for about 1–2 minutes on each side or until golden brown on both sides. Remove from heat and set aside (chicken will not be cooked yet, but will cook later in the sauce).

3. Reduce heat to medium and add onion to the pan and cook for 3–4 minutes, until soft and translucent. Add garlic, mushrooms, and a pinch of salt to the pan and cook for about 2–3 more minutes, until mushrooms release juices and they are mostly cooked off.

4. Add Marsala, chicken stock, and chicken and simmer for about 10 more minutes, or until chicken is cooked through and sauce thickens slightly. If sauce does not thicken as much as you would like, mix cornstarch and 2 teaspoon water in a separate bowl until cornstarch dissolves. Add this mixture to the simmering liquid and simmer for another minute.

5   While sauce is simmering, cook egg noodles according
    to directions on box. Drain and toss with butter and
    set aside.

6   Serve by placing a chicken breast on each plate, and
    spooning sauce over each chicken breast. Divide pasta
    in half and place on the side of each plate.

Chicken Stock and Chicken Broth

Some of our recipes call for chicken stock
or chicken broth. What's the difference?
Generally, chicken stock is made from only
or mostly chicken bones, which have a high
gelatin content. When bones are simmered
with water and cooked down, this gelatin
becomes part of the stock and it can thicken
it considerably. This is great for a nice thick
sauce but not necessarily for soup. Chicken
broth, on the other hand, is cooked with
some chicken bones and lots of chicken
meat, so it gets the same rich flavor but
doesn't thicken nearly as much.

There are many options out there, including
powdered, liquid, and concentrates. Don't
worry too much about stock vs. broth, since
most store-bought versions use the words
interchangeably. We recommend a store-
bought concentrate (it looks almost like a
paste), but the most important thing is that
whichever you buy only contains natural
ingredients, and no artificial additives or
preservatives.

Fettuccine with Shrimp Scampi

Eli: Shrimp Scampi reminds me of the years I spent attending various black tie events. Silver hors d'oeuvres trays, servers wearing bow ties and an awesome DJ who was probably about 10 years too old to still be working. If you can't find a bow tie, this Shrimp Scampi will have to do in order to impress your dinner guests. There was one lesson I did learn about how to impress your guests from attending all those parties — preparing a choreographed dance routine will leave everyone at the party wanting more. And just like any good party should...this dish will leave your guests wanting more.

Cooking to Impress

Main Course

Serves 2

Total time 30 minutes

½ pound dry **fettuccine**

3 tablespoons extra virgin **olive oil**

10 jumbo **shrimp**, shelled and deveined (see Kitchen Tip: Thawing Shrimp, page 64)

salt and **pepper**

¼ cup finely chopped **shallot** or **onion**

2 medium cloves **garlic**, minced

¼ cup dry **white wine**

¼ cup **chicken stock**

1 tablespoon freshly squeezed **lemon juice**

2 tablespoons **unsalted butter** or **Herb Butter**, page 126

¼ cup finely chopped **parsley**, for garnish

1. Cook pasta according to the directions on the box. Drain, then toss with 2 tablespoons olive oil and set aside.

2. Season the shrimp by sprinkling lightly with salt and pepper.

3. Toss the shrimp in a hot nonstick skillet with 1 tablespoon olive oil.

4. Cook until browned on both sides, about 1 minute on each side.

5. Add shallot or onion and garlic and sauté until soft and fragrant, about 1–2 minutes.

6. Add white wine and chicken broth, bring to a simmer, and cook for 5 more minutes.

7. Turn off heat and toss in the Herb Butter and lemon juice.

8. Add the pasta, and toss until evenly coated.

9. Garnish with parsley and serve.

Chicken with Sun-dried Tomato and Artichokes

This is a great go-to when you need an elegant dish to serve and it takes minimal prep work. The sun-dried tomatoes look great and deliver a richer, more intense flavor than using fresh whole tomatoes. Keeping the artichokes and sun-dried tomatoes moist and out of the sauté means their flavors stay bright and fresh. If your sun-dried tomatoes start off very dry, re-hydrate them by soaking in 1 cup of hot water for 10 minutes.

Cooking to Impress

 Main Course

 Serves 2

Total time 30 minutes

1 jar (14 ounce) marinated **artichokes**, drained

12 ounces sun-dried **tomatoes**, rehydrated if necessary

1 large clove **garlic**, thinly sliced

1 tablespoon chopped **parsley**

1–2 **lemons**, juiced (should have around 2–3 tablespoons)

3 tablespoons extra virgin **olive oil**, divided

salt and **pepper** to taste

2 large boneless **chicken breasts**

Linguine and Herbs, page 81

Sautéed Spinach, page 116

1 Mix together artichokes, sun-dried tomatoes, garlic, parsley, lemon juice, and 1 tablespoon olive oil. Set aside.

2 Heat remaining olive oil in a nonstick frying pan on medium-high.

3 Season chicken with salt and pepper, then add chicken, reduce heat to medium and sauté until chicken is cooked through, about 4 minutes on each side.

4 Turn off the heat and place chicken on a plate. Spoon desired amount of the artichoke mixture on top of each breast.

5 Serve with Linguine and Herbs and Sautéed Spinach.

Herb Butter

Cooking to Impress

 Prep

 Yields ½ cup

 Prep time 5–10 minutes

1 stick **salted butter**
½ teaspoon fresh finely chopped **chives**
½ teaspoon fresh finely chopped **oregano**
½ teaspoon fresh finely chopped **thyme**
½ teaspoon fresh finely chopped **rosemary**

1   Let butter soften at room temperature for 1 hour.

2   When the butter is soft, add the herbs.

3   Blend until herbs are fully mixed.

Cutting Fresh Herbs

The vibrant and intense flavors of fresh herbs often don't compare with their dried counterparts, especially in a recipe like this where they occupy such a prominent role. But cutting fresh herbs to bring them to their highest potential can be tricky.

For rosemary, oregano, and thyme, remove small leaves from the stem. Try pinching the stem between your index finger and thumb and sliding down the stem. Most of the leaves should be stripped right off. You can go back and remove remaining leaves individually. Then finely chop the leaves.

For basil, remove leaves from the stem, and stack on top of one another. Then roll the stack of leaves the long way into a tight roll. Slice thin strips off the roll (this is called chiffonade, if you want to impress your friends).

For chives, line up about 10 and cut very thin slices from all of them at the same time. Chives bruise easily so cut them thin the first time and then don't try to cut them again.

Homemade Breadcrumbs

While store-bought breadcrumbs will often suffice, when the flavor of breadcrumbs is prominent you will want to make them from scratch.

Cooking to Impress

 Prep

 Yields approximately ⅓ cup, depending on size of bread

 Total time 35 minutes

5–6 slices good **Italian bread**

1   Preheat oven to 275°F.

2   Bake bread for 10–15 minutes, until it has dried out. Let bread cool.

3   Break up bread slices and then process in food processor until bread reaches a fine crumb consistency.

4   Store in airtight container or zip-close bag. Will stay for several days, or you can freeze for up to a month.

Penne with Greens and Spicy Italian Sausage

Max: I love cooking greens, and you can use any kind you like in this recipe. Tougher greens like kale or collards will need to be simmered longer at the end, while chard or spinach cooks in a minute or two.

This dish is light enough for lunch and filling enough for dinner—and there's no tomato sauce, so it's a welcome change from the pasta norm.

Cooking to Impress

Main Course

Serves 4

Total time 30 minutes

1 pound dry **penne pasta**

3 tablespoons extra virgin **olive oil**

1 bunch **kale**, **collard greens**, or **Swiss chard**

2 hot **Italian sausages**

½ cup diced **onion**, ½-inch pieces

2 cloves **garlic**, thinly sliced

½ **jalapeño** (de-seeded) or **hot Hungarian pepper**, minced (use more if you like spicy)

¾ cup dry **white wine**

1 tablespoon **butter**

salt and **pepper** to taste

1. Cook pasta according to directions on box. Drain and toss with 2 tablespoons olive oil and set aside.

2. Meanwhile, wash and rinse the greens. Remove the stems and then coarsely chop or tear the greens and set aside.

3. Heat a nonstick skillet with 1 tablespoon olive oil until smoking.

4a. For raw sausage, remove the sausage from their casings, and add to the pan. Sauté on high until browned. Remove from heat and set aside.

4b. For pre-cooked sausage, slice and add to the pan. Sauté on high until browned.

5. Reduce heat to medium-high. If the pan looks dry add a bit of oil. Add onions and hot peppers and a pinch of salt and sauté for 3–5 minutes or until onions are soft. Add garlic and sauté for another minute. Add white wine and cook until half the liquid is gone.

6. Add greens and simmer until tender, about 2 minutes for chard, and 5–7 minutes for kale or collards (you might have to add some more water for the kale or collards). Turn off heat, add in butter and stir until melts in. Season with salt and pepper to taste.

7. Add penne and stir until combined evenly and serve.

129

Homemade Roasted Red Pepper

Max: You can spend quite a bit of money on roasted red peppers in the store or, if you have 20 minutes, you can make them yourself. You can easily make these in the oven or the gas grill, depending on where you're going to be cooking dinner. It's wise to get a pair of tongs ready for either technique.

Roasted Red Pepper is a perfect complement to the Salmon Goat Cheese Napoleon, page 132, although it can be served by itself as a side dish. Mixing it with a rice pilaf or a couscous makes a great accompaniment with a meat dish.

Cooking to Impress

 Prep

 Yields 4 roasted red peppers

 Total time 20 minutes

4 large **red peppers**
extra virgin **olive oil**
salt

In the Oven

1   Preheat an oven to broiling or 450°F for 20 minutes.

2   Spread a few tablespoons of olive oil on each pepper using your hand. Sprinkle a dash of salt on each pepper.

3   Place peppers on a cookie sheet lined with parchment paper or aluminum foil.

4   Broil for 15–20 minutes, turning about every 5 minutes. Peppers should be about half charred and half still red.

5   Remove from oven and place peppers in an airtight container, or bowl covered with plastic wrap for 10 minutes.

6   Remove peppers and peel under running water, removing skin, seeds, and interior.

On a Gas Grill or Range

1. Place whole red pepper on grill or right above the flame on a gas range.
2. When the skin turns black, turn the pepper ¼ turn. Repeat until the entire pepper's skin is charred and almost entirely black.
3. Repeat for each pepper.
4. Remove from oven and place peppers in an airtight container, or bowl covered with plastic wrap for 10 minutes.
5. Remove peppers and peel under running water, removing skin, seeds, and interior.
6. See Marinating Peppers, below.

Marinating Peppers

Marinating the peppers adds flavor and also lets you store them longer. Place peppers in airtight container and cover in kosher salt, extra virgin olive oil, white wine vinegar, whole garlic cloves, and fresh springs of thyme, oregano, and/or rosemary. Seal container and put in refrigerate. Should keep for 1–2 weeks.

Salmon and Goat Cheese Napoleon

 Main Course

 Serves 2

 Total time 45 minutes

10 ounces **salmon filet**

pinch **salt** and **pepper**

½ teaspoon **thyme**

½ teaspoon **dill**

2 tablespoons extra virgin or
    blended **olive oil**

1 **zucchini**

2 cloves minced **garlic**

2 tablespoons finely chopped fresh **chives**

1 Roasted **Red Pepper**, page 130

¼ pound **goat cheese** (Chèvre)

Wild Rice Pilaf, page 83

1   Season salmon by sprinkling it with the salt, pepper, thyme, and dill.

2   Heat olive oil in a nonstick frying pan and cook salmon on medium for 10 minutes, turning over halfway through.

3   Cut zucchini in half width-wise, then in thin slices lengthwise. Sauté or grill until tender with the garlic and chives.

4   Cut Roasted Red Pepper, goat cheese, and salmon to match zucchini slices.

5   Layer salmon, goat cheese, zucchini, and roasted red pepper to form a tower. Secure with toothpick if necessary.

6   Serve with Wild Rice Pilaf.

This dish emerged from a combination of two of my favorite flavors. The rich flavor of the roasted salmon and vegetables pairs so perfectly with the sharp flavor of the goat cheese. Stacking a dish is a quick and not too difficult way to show off the different colors and components of this dish.

Stuffed Mushrooms

There is this unbelievably catchy Jock Jams™ song that goes "We like to party! We like! We like to party! We like to party! We're gonna have a party and everybody's dancin'!! There's gonna be a party! And everybody's comin'!!" (C'mon, you know that you know it...) Well have a party, make these mushrooms, play that song and see what happens. We guarantee results. And we want to be invited because that party sounds amazing.

Cooking to Impress

 Side Dish

 Serves 4

 Total time 20 minutes

30 **button mushrooms**
3 tablespoons **butter**, or **Herb Butter**, page 126
½ cup **Italian breadcrumbs**, or **Homemade Breadcrumbs**, page 128
2 tablespoons **Worcestershire sauce**
Parmesan cheese, grated

1 Wash and hollow out the mushrooms. Save the stems.

2 Dice the stems very small but not into a mushy mess. Make sure they are still pieces, just small.

3 Melt 3 tablespoons butter in a pan.

4 Mix in the mushroom stems with the butter, the breadcrumbs and Worcestershire sauce.

5 Fill the hollowed out mushrooms with this mixture. Cover a baking sheet with aluminum foil and place mushrooms stuffed side up.

6 Lightly sprinkle the mushrooms with Parmesan cheese.

7 Cook at 350°F until cheese melts and mushrooms are golden brown.

8 Serve immediately. Add more Parmesan cheese if desired.

Sesame-Soy Salmon

Out of the dozens of great dishes our mom prepared on a regular basis, this meal always stands out in our memory and we figured we could make it too. The soy sauce and sesame oil work really well with the fish; they never overpower each other, leaving both flavors shining through.

Cooking to Impress

Main Course

Serves 2

Total time 40 minutes

---

1 tablespoon **vegetable oil**

1 tablespoon minced **shallot** or **onion**

1 tablespoon minced **ginger**

½ cup **rice wine** or **dry white wine**

2 teaspoons **brown sugar**

1 tablespoon **lime juice**

2 tablespoons **soy sauce**

1 tablespoon **sesame oil**

2 (7 ounce) pieces **salmon filet**

olive oil

salt and **pepper**

2 tablespoons **vegetable oil**

1 teaspoon toasted **sesame seeds**

Grilled Zucchini and Yellow Squash, page 108

For Sauce

1   Heat oil in a saucepan until shimmering.

2   Add shallot, ginger, and garlic, and cook on low for 10 minutes.

3   Add rice wine or white wine, brown sugar, and lime juice and simmer until reduced by half or thickened slightly.

4   Turn off heat and add soy sauce and sesame oil. Set aside.

For salmon

1   Heat oven to 350°F.

2   Brush salmon with olive oil and sprinkle evenly with salt and pepper.

3   Heat 2 tablespoons vegetable oil until barely smoking in ovenproof frying pan. Place fish, topside down in pan and brown for 1 minute. Flip and brown the other side for 1 minute.

4   Move frying pan into oven and cook for 5–8 minutes. Test for doneness by gently squeezing the sides of the fish. When they feel firm but not tough or hard the fish is done.

5   Place the salmon on a plate and pour 2 tablespoons of the sauce over it and garnish with toasted sesame seeds. Serve with Grilled Zucchini and Yellow Squash.

Themed Meals

You made it. NO wait...we made it. Together. This has been good hasn't it? We should do this again sometime. Yeah, our e-mail's in the back, and that's the best way to get in touch with us. We'd really like to hear your thoughts and ideas on any recipes in this cookbook or any you wished we had put in. By the way, we wanted to let you know that you are such a great cook now. We are really proud. And yes, you are welcome, but really all we did was instruct you step by step to get you to where you are right now, so you know, no big deal.

This chapter is like the final test but with no grades. You could try to make all of these items alone but you might want some help. We suggest you invite some friends over. You can be the chef and teach them how to cook a dish from start to finish.

We've organized three delicious several course meals. For each themed meal you can find more pictures and visuals online at www.freshmaninthekitchen.com. Feel free to contact us about what other types of additions you made to these multi-course meals. We know we are scratching the surface of what these cuisines can offer, so hopefully the recipes will encourage you to research deeper.

Dishes from the **Mediterranean** area make up some of our all-time favorites. In this cuisine, aromatic spices deliver flavors that are unique and incomparable. For our feast we have a lemony lentil soup, delicious homemade hummus with pita, our version of the Middle-Eastern classic Chicken Shawarma, and a yogurt dill sauce called Tzatziki to top it all off.

The second feast in this chapter is **Italian**. Yes, we own a map, and yes, we know Italy is in the Mediterranean. We love the food so much that we just had to give Italian food its own section. Everyone has eaten Italian food, but home-cooked Italian is so filling and rich that you might never go out again. These are the classics. Spaghetti and large meatballs with an antipasto salad bursting with fresh veggies and a homemade dressing, buttery hot garlic bread and a rich vegetable minestrone soup.

The last meal is **Japanese** inspired. Sushi is really hot right now, and very healthy. Basically everyone is doing it. Making sushi isn't as difficult as it looks. As a matter of fact, once you get the right ingredients and the technique down it is so simple and you can start making up your own rolls! To complement the sushi rolls, we have Miso Soup, a traditional accompaniment to sushi, Goma Ae, a Japanese spinach salad, and Yakisoba, the Japanese stir-fry.

Tzatziki

Eli: This can be used for dipping vegetables, as a sauce for salads and meats, and goes great with the Chicken Schwarma (page 140). This is a variation on the way we made it at the Greek restaurant I worked at during college. This way is delicious and has a few more steps that really antes up the flavor.

Themed Meals

Side Dish

Yields 1 cup

Total time 10 minutes

1 cup **yogurt** or **sour cream**

2 cloves **garlic**, minced

1 tablespoon finely chopped fresh **dill**

1 tablespoon extra virgin **olive oil**

¼ **cucumber**, peeled

salt and **pepper**

1. Mix the yogurt or sour cream, garlic, dill, and olive oil in a large bowl.

2. Cut the cucumber into quarters (like pickle spears). Remove all the seeds. You can use a spoon to scrape the seeds out.

3. Grate the cucumber into a small bowl. Holding the bowl in one hand, use your other hand to press against the cucumber draining the excess water. Try to get as much water out of the cucumber as you can. You should have about ¼-cup of cucumber at this point. Mix the grated cucumber into the sour cream mixture.

4. Season with salt and pepper to taste, and allow to rest in the fridge minimum two hours before serving.

Chicken Shawarma

As the famous saying goes "This ain't your parents Shawarma." Here's our spin on the middle-eastern favorite. The Homemade Hummus and Tomato, Onion, and Cucumber Salad add a lot of flavor to the pita sandwich so don't leave them out.

Themed Meals

 Main Course

 Serves 4

 Prep time 45 minutes/Total time 60 minutes

Shawarma

1 pound boneless **chicken thighs**
3 **garlic** cloves, minced
1 tablespoon **cumin**
1 teaspoon **paprika**
¼ teaspoon **cayenne pepper**
1 tablespoon **lemon juice**
salt and **pepper**
3 tablespoons extra virgin **olive oil**

Accompaniments

pita bread
Homemade Hummus, page 38
Tomato, Onion and Cucumber Salad,
    page 41

1   Dice chicken thighs to ½-inch pieces.

2   Mix remaining ingredients together. Toss in chicken and mix so that chicken is coated well in the spice mixture. Let stand for at least 30 minutes and up to 24 hours in refrigerator (the longer the better).

3   Heat a nonstick skillet to medium-high heat.

4   Add chicken and cook until chicken is browned and cooked through, about 6–7 minutes. Remove from heat.

5   Spread a thin layer of Hummus on a piece of pita bread. Add cooked chicken and a few spoonfuls of Tomato, Onion, and Cucumber Salad. Roll up and enjoy!

Lentil Soup

2 tablespoons extra virgin **olive oil**

1 cup diced **onion**, ¼-inch pieces

2 cloves **garlic**

1 inch **ginger** root, minced (optional)

1 pound **dry red lentils**

8 cups **chicken broth**, **vegetable broth**, or **water**

½ cup **lemon juice**

2 teaspoons **cumin**

salt and **pepper**

2 tablespoons finely chopped **parsley**

As you may have noticed throughout our cookbook, we love our soups. Maybe it was all those frigid Michigan winters growing up that necessitated keeping a hot bowl of soup close by. This lentil soup is best enjoyed with some warm pita bread on the side.

1   Heat the oil in a soup pot on medium. When it's hot, add the onion, garlic, and ginger (if using) and sauté until onion releases liquid and it is cooked off, about 10 minutes.

2   Add the lentils and chicken stock or water. Bring to a boil and reduce heat so that the soup is just simmering. Simmer for 30 minutes or until lentils break down.

3   Add lemon juice, cumin, and salt and pepper to taste. Mix well. Ladle into bowls and garnish generously with parsley.

Minestrone Soup

Themed Meals

 Soup

 Serves 6

 Prep Time 15 minutes/Total time 60 minutes

2 tablespoons **olive oil**

1 cup diced **celery**, ½-inch pieces

1 cup diced **carrots**, 1–2-inch pieces

1 cup diced **onion**, ¼-inch pieces

3 cloves **garlic**, minced

2 cans (15 ounces each) **stewed tomatoes**

3 cups chicken or **vegetable broth**

3 cups **water**

2 teaspoons finely chopped fresh **oregano**

2 teaspoons finely chopped or chiffonade
   fresh **basil** (see Cutting Herbs, page 127)

1 can (15 ounce) **garbanzo** or **kidney beans**

⅓ cup finely chopped **parsley**

½ cup **orzo pasta**

½ cup diced **potato**, ¾-inch pieces

salt and **pepper** to taste

Parmesan cheese

1 tablespoon finely chopped **parsley**

1 Heat olive oil on medium-high in a large pot. When hot, add celery, carrots, and onion. Cook until juices are released and cooked off, about 8 minutes.

2 Add garlic, stewed tomatoes, broth, water, oregano, and basil. Bring to a boil then simmer for 20 minutes.

3 Add the beans, parsley, pasta and potatoes. Cook 15 minutes.

4 Season with salt and pepper to taste. Ladle into bowls and garnish with Parmesan cheese and parsley.

Similar to our feelings on many store-bought salad dressings, we don't advocate buying canned soup either. This minestrone soup will convince you to skip the canned soups aisle at your supermarket forever.

Why does spaghetti and meatballs often get the kids menu moniker at restaurants? We just don't get it. Well, here's our version to make in your home and perfect for any age range, enough to feed the kids, the friends, the whole family or a small army.

If you've made it this far you might be asking yourself why this recipe calls for blending whole tomatoes in a food processor, instead of just buying crushed tomatoes. In our opinion you can really tell the difference. The difference is the amount of processing. Whole peeled tomatoes have been processed less than the crushed tomatoes and you can see and taste the difference. Try it out if you want, buy a can of crushed tomatoes and a can of whole tomatoes that you have blended and taste them both.

Spaghetti with Marinara Sauce and Meatballs

Themed Meals

Main Course

Serves 8

Total time 1 hour

Homemade Marinara Sauce

2 cans (16 ounces each) whole peeled
   tomatoes
3 tablespoons extra virgin **olive oil**
¾ cup diced **onion**, ¼-inch pieces
3 tablespoons minced **garlic**
2 large sprigs of fresh **basil**, around
   4 ounces
salt and **pepper** to taste
2 pounds dry **spaghetti**
3 tablespoons extra virgin olive oil
Baby Meatballs, page 51
Parmesan Cheese
1 tablespoon finely chopped parsley

1   Put whole peeled tomatoes with their juice in a food processor and process until blended. Set aside.

2   Heat the olive oil on medium-high. When it's hot, add the onions and sauté until they release their juices and they cook off, about 7 minutes.

3   Add the garlic and sauté for 1 minute only.

4   Add the tomatoes and basil. Submerge the basil under the sauce, bring to a simmer, and cook on low for 20 minutes.

5   Meanwhile, cook spaghetti according to directions on box. Drain and toss with olive oil. Set aside in a warm place.

6   When pasta and sauce are cooked, check sauce and season to taste with salt and pepper.

7   Place spaghetti in bowls, ladle sauce over and set meatballs on top. Garnish with Parmesan Cheese and parsley.

Timesaver: If you have time and want to make something really special, make both the meatballs and sauce from scratch. If you are short on time, make only one from scratch and buy the other one prepared.

Antipasto Salad

Themed Meals

 Salad

 Serves 4–6

 Total time here

2 large heads **Romaine lettuce**, washed and dried

1 can (12 ounce) pitted **Kalamata olives**

1 can (12 ounce) **artichoke hearts**

1 can (12 ounce) sliced **beets**

8–10 **pepperoncini**

1 large **green pepper**, sliced into rings

¼ pound **provolone cheese**, cubed

¼ pound **spicy salami**, sliced thin

¼ pound **pepperoni**, sliced thin

¼ pound thick sliced **Italian ham**, cubed

2 large **tomatoes**

Dressing

½ cup extra virgin **olive oil**

⅓ cup **red wine vinegar**

1 teaspoon **garlic powder**

1 tablespoon fresh **basil**

1 tablespoon fresh **oregano**

salt and **pepper** to taste

Eli: This adapted salad recipe can be found at Detroit area Coney Islands and at a restaurant I worked at in college. We took the original and added our own spin to make it even more flavorful. Served with pizza or pasta, it's a success every time.

1. Chop the Romaine and place in a large bowl.

2. Drain the olives, artichoke hearts and beets. Add to the bowl.

3. Add the pepperoncini, green pepper, cheese and meats to the bowl.

4. Slice the tomato into halves. Cut into 1-inch pieces. Add to the bowl.

5. In a separate bowl, combine the dressing ingredients. Whisk well with a fork. Pour over the salad. Toss and serve.

Garlic Bread

4 tablespoons **butter**
2 large cloves **garlic**, minced
1 large **baguette**
¼ cup **Parmesan cheese**

Only one rule applies: get great fresh bread, end up with delicious garlic bread.

1 Preheat oven to 400°F.

2 Melt the butter over medium-low heat in a small pan. Add the garlic and remove from heat.

3 Slice the baguette lengthwise like a hot dog bun, then into 2-inch pieces. Lay open face up on a cookie sheet.

4 Using a pastry brush, brush the bread slices with the garlic butter, making sure to get some pieces of garlic on each slice.

5 Sprinkle Parmesan cheese evenly over each slice.

6 Cook in the oven for 5–10 minutes, or until golden brown.

Miso Soup

This is the soup that most likely came to your table before your sushi arrived at your favorite Japanese restaurant. Feel free to break with tradition and add some carrot, cabbage, celery, or any other vegetable in your fridge. We suggest going to a Japanese grocery for the most authentic ingredients, but these days, your local supermarket will probably carry everything you need.

Themed Meals

 Soup

 Serves 4

Total time 25 minutes

6 cups **water**

½ pound diced **tofu**, ½-inch pieces

2 tablespoons dried **wakame seaweed**

1 teaspoon **dashi powder** (optional)

2 tablespoons **miso paste**

2–3 **green onions**, thinly sliced

1   Boil the 6 cups water in a medium size pot.

2   Reduce heat to low and add tofu, wakame, and dashi.

3   Turn heat off and add miso paste, stirring to dissolve.

4   Garnish with green onions and serve.

Sushi

This recipe will explain how to make sushi with some basic fillings. The key to sushi is the rice. It must be not too hard and not too soft. Once you get that down, you can start to try out different fillings. Don't get carried away with piling in too many fillings, or it won't close up properly.

Themed Meals

 Main Course

 Yields 6–8 rolls

 Total time 40

Sushi Rice

1 ½ cups **Japanese sushi rice or short-grained white rice**

2 ¾ cups **water**

¼ cup **seasoned rice vinegar**

Filling

1 **carrot**, thinly sliced

1 **cucumber**, thinly sliced

1 **avocado**, thinly sliced

8 sheets **nori**

bamboo sushi roller

1. In a rice cooker or heavy pot, add rice and water and bring to a boil. Reduce heat to very low and cook until water is absorbed, about 15–20 minutes.

2. When rice is done, remove from heat and gently mix in vinegar with rubber spatula.

3. Spread the rice out onto a cookie sheet to cool. Wait until it is no longer hot (but it does not have to be cold). You can use this time to prepare your filling.

4. Place a nori sheet on the bamboo sushi roller with the longer end facing you. Get a bowl of water and moisten your hands to prevent rice from sticking to them. Using your moistened hands spread enough rice to cover the bottom ½ of the nori to about ¼-inch thickness. Dip your hands in the water to re-moisten them periodically. Make sure the rice is spread evenly and to the edges.

5 Place 2–3 pieces each of carrot, cucumber, and avocado across the center of the rice (the vegetables should be in a straight line going from left to right). Press them down gently.

6 Roll up the sushi roll, starting with the end nearest to you. Roll the end nearest you to meet the spot where the rice ends. You should have a 2–3 inch area of plain nori. Brush some water there to moisten the nori, then continue to roll, pressing gently to seal.

7 Slice the nori into 8 pieces, using a very sharp knife. Moisten the knife with water between each slice (keep a tall glass of water handy), and wipe the knife clean, re-moistening every 2–3 cuts.

Note on rice vinegar

There are two types of rice vinegar, seasoned and unseasoned. Seasoned rice vinegar has sugar and salt dissolved in it, while unseasoned has nothing besides vinegar. For this recipe, since we want the sugar and salt in the rice, we use seasoned rice vinegar. If you have unseasoned vinegar, while the rice is cooking, dissolve 1 teaspoon granulated sugar and ½ teaspoon salt in the vinegar and bring to a boil, mixing to dissolve. Remove from heat and proceed with the recipe.

Spicy Mayonnaise

Absolutely necessary for spicy tuna and spicy salmon rolls, and delicious on just about any other roll as well.

Themed Meals

 Prep

 Yields ½ cup

 Total time 5 minutes

½ cup **mayonnaise**

1–2 teaspoons **Sriracha chili sauce** (available in Asian section of grocery store or Asian market)

Mix mayonnaise and Sriracha together. Add more mayonnaise or Sriracha to desired level of spiciness.

Sushi Filling Ideas
Imitation Crab
Crab Meat
Sashimi-grade Fish: Tuna, Salmon, Yellow Tail, Eel, Mackerel
Green Onion
Avocado
Fried Tofu
Cucumber

Inside-Out Rolls
If you want to impress people with your sushi skills, follow these directions to make a beautiful inside-out roll.

Cover the bamboo roller in plastic wrap, wrapping in both directions so that no part of the roller is exposed. Spread rice 2/3 up the roll. Once the rice is spread out, flip the roll over so that the end with no rice on it is close to you and on the underside. Place filling there and roll up.

This is a slightly different kind of spinach salad than you might have had before. The spinach is first cooked very quickly, giving it a deep green color. The sweetness of the brown sugar perfectly balances the rich flavor of the sesame oil.

Goma Ae
(Spinach Salad)

Themed Meals

Salad

Serves 2–4

Total time 15 minutes

3 tablespoons **soy sauce**

1 tablespoon **brown sugar**

1 ½ tablespoons toasted **sesame oil**

1 bag (10 ounce) **baby spinach**

1 teaspoon **sesame seeds**

1 Mix together soy sauce, brown sugar, and toasted sesame oil in a large bowl until sugar dissolves.

2 Bring a medium pot of water to a boil.

3 Submerge spinach in boiling water for 1 minute.

4 Drain into a colander and immediately rinse in cold water. Use your hands to press all the water out of the spinach.

5 Add the spinach to the bowl and toss with sauce. Transfer to serving dish and garnish by sprinkling with sesame seeds.

Yakisoba

Themed Meals

 Main Course

 Serves 4

 Prep time 15 minutes/Total time 40 minutes

Noodles

½ pound fresh or frozen **Yakisoba noodles** (thin wheat noodles, available at Asian markets or in Asian section of grocery stores)

1 tablespoon **vegetable oil**, more as needed

Chicken

1 tablespoon **vegetable oil**

½ pound diced boneless **chicken breast**, **pork tenderloin**, or **tofu** (see note on pressing tofu, page 90), ½-inch pieces

1 tablespoon **soy sauce**

1 tablespoon **mirin** (sweet rice wine, available at Asian markets or in Asian section of grocery stores)

This is a lot like Lo Mein. If you can't find Yakisoba noodles at your local Asian grocery, try using ramen noodles.

For the Noodles

1   Cook noodles according to directions on the box, drain and set aside (some Yakisoba noodles cook very quickly, so make sure not to overcook them).

2   If they will be resting for more than 5 minutes, toss with some vegetable oil so that they don't stick together.

For the Meat

Heat oil, preferably in a wok, otherwise use a nonstick skillet, and add chicken. Cook, tossing occasionally, until chicken is browned on all sides. Add soy sauce and mirin and cook for 2 more minutes. Remove chicken and set aside.

Peeling and Mincing Ginger

Ginger is a very firm, very flavorful root found in many Asian cuisines. Because of its texture, it can be intimidating, but it's really no different than cutting other vegetables, though it does help to have a sharp knife. To peel ginger, use an ordinary teaspoon and scrape along the outside of the ginger with the tip of the spoon until all skin is removed. To mince ginger (mince meaning cut very small), first slice into slices (see Kitchen Technique: Dicing and Chopping, page 25). Then cut these slices into long strips. Lastly, line up a few strips at a time and cut them into very small pieces.

Vegetables

2 tablespoons **vegetable oil**

1 diced **carrot**, ½-inch pieces

½ diced **onion**, ½-inch pieces

1 cup diced **cabbage**, ¾-inch pieces

½ cup diced **celery**, ½-inch pieces

2 cloves **garlic**, minced

1 inch **ginger**, minced

3 tablespoons **soy sauce**

1–2 teaspoons Sriracha or other **chili sauce**

1 tablespoon **mirin** (sweet rice wine)

1 teaspoon **sesame oil**

For the Vegetables

1 Wipe or clean out wok or skillet. Add vegetable oil to skillet on high heat. Add carrot, onion, cabbage, celery, garlic, and ginger and cook until vegetables are just tender, 3–4 minutes.

2 Add soy sauce, chili paste, mirin, and sesame oil, and toss to combine. Add noodles and chicken back to pan and cook for 1–2 more minutes, until everything is hot and evenly coated with sauce.

3 Season to taste with more Sriracha and soy sauce and serve.

Des

We close out our cookbook the same as we would any great meal — with dessert.

We like to use fruit and natural sweets to create confections that will leave you upbeat and ready to hit the town instead of tired and ready to hit the sack. We have some old classics and a few twists on your favorite after-dinner treats. Remember that desserts should complement the meal, not overshadow it.

We both advocate eating dessert at any time of the day so if anybody asks you why you are stuffing your face with cake at 9 am, we'll take the blame. Just tell them in between bites that Max and Eli made you do it and it's too good to stop. Offer them a bite (if you can spare some and are in a giving mood) and then they will surely understand.

serts

Angel Food Cake with Fresh Strawberry Topping

The strawberries are naturally sweet so don't go too heavy on the sauce. Adding a scoop of vanilla ice cream or a light sorbet is a perfect summer addition.

Desserts

 Dessert

 Serves 4

 Total time 20 minutes

1 **angel food cake** (13 ounce)
About 30 **strawberries**, cleaned and tops
   removed
1 tablespoon **sugar**
1 tablespoon **water**
whipped cream (optional)

1 Bring the water, sugar, and half the strawberries to a boil in a small saucepan. Reduce heat to low and simmer for 10 minutes.

2 Cut the angel food cake into slices and plate.

3 Pour a small amount of the cooked strawberry sauce over the slice. Serve immediately with a portion of the remaining strawberries and whipped cream.

Extremely fast, simple and light, this dessert is great for topping off a meal where you don't want to be weighed down later in the night.

Apple Crisp

Eli: Almost every time Max goes off the top of his head to create a recipe, it floors me. I tasted this apple crisp and was speechless. It was so good it knocked both my shoes and socks off. And the shoes were double knotted. It's not very labor intensive and uses affordable and accessible ingredients. To give it a real 4-star restaurant flair, serve it hot with a side of vanilla ice cream with warm caramel drizzled over the top.

Desserts

Dessert

Serves 8–10

Prep Time 20 minutes/Total time 1 hour 20 minutes

10–12 **Granny Smith apples**, enough to generously fill a 9x13 baking dish

¼ cup **brown sugar**

¼ cup **flour**

1 cup **unsalted butter**, melted

2 cups **all-purpose flour**

2 cups **oatmeal**

2 cups **brown sugar**

1 tablespoon **cinnamon**

½ teaspoon **cloves**

1 Preheat an oven to 350°F.

2 Chop the apples to bite size pieces, about 1-inch.

3 Toss the apples with brown sugar and flour and set aside.

4 In a large bowl, pour the melted butter over the 2 cups flour, oatmeal, brown sugar, cinnamon and cloves and mix well.

5 Pour the apples into a 9x13 baking dish.

6 Press the flour mix into biscuit shapes and evenly place over the apple. Press down so that the flour mix is firm, not crumbly or powdery.

7 Bake until topping is golden brown and apples are bubbling, about 45 minutes to 1 hour.

Ultimate Chocolate Fudge Cake with Mocha Buttercream Frosting

Eli: This cake reigns supreme. Cake baking is quite an endeavor, but for a decadent finish to a perfect meal, nothing can top that slice of rich, moist, fresh, chocolate cake. (For that matter, the leftover cake makes an excellent breakfast the next morning.) For this cake, as with all baking, be patient and don't rush it, especially the frosting. However, if you make a mistake, you will still likely have a pile of rich chocolaty goodness in one form or another, so no need to worry.

Desserts

 Dessert

 Serves 8–10

 Prep Time: 40 minutes/Cooking Time: 60 minutes

6 ounces **unsweetened chocolate**

2 cups **all-purpose flour**

1 teaspoon **baking soda**

¼ teaspoon **salt**

¼ pound **unsalted butter**

½ pound **granulated sugar**

½ pound **brown sugar**

2 **eggs**

1 teaspoon **vanilla**

¼ cup **sour cream**

1 ½ cup **milk**

1 tablespoon **instant coffee**

Mocha Buttercream Frosting
   (recipe following)

1   Grease a 10-inch cake or spring-form pan and line the bottom with parchment paper. Preheat the oven to 350°F.

2   Melt the chocolate over a double boiler or in the microwave, taking care not to burn the chocolate. Set aside.

3   Mix together the flour, baking soda, and salt, and set aside.

4   Mix the butter and sugars in a large mixing bowl until light and fluffy.

5   Add the eggs, one at a time, mixing each egg in completely before adding the next.

6   Stir in the vanilla, then mix in the melted chocolate.

7   Add ⅓ of the dry ingredients and mix to combine.

8   Mix together the sour cream, milk, and coffee powder, and add half to the bowl, mix to combine.

9   Add half the remaining dry ingredients, then the remaining milk mixture, and then the remaining dry ingredients. Stir to combine.

10 Pour into the prepared pan. Spread batter to sides with rubber spatula. Bake for 45–60 minutes, until a toothpick inserted into the center of the cake comes out clean.

Mocha Buttercream Frosting

This frosting is a perfect complement to the cake. To help with the frosting process, wait until the cake has cooled completely before frosting. If not, the heat of the cake will melt the frosting right off. It is best to wrap the cake in plastic wrap and freeze it for 30 minutes before frosting. The key is having a cool cake and room temperature frosting.

Desserts

Dessert

Covers Ultimate Chocolate Fudge Cake

Frosting Time: 30 minutes

1 cup **unsalted butter** at room temperature
4 cups **powdered sugar**
1 teaspoon **vanilla extract**
2 tablespoons **coffee powder**
2–3 tablespoons **milk** or **heavy cream**

1 Mix all ingredients except cream together in food processor on high until blended.

2 Add enough cream until frosting reaches spreadable consistency.

3 Dip a rubber or offset spatula in water and use it to frost the cake, dipping the spatula in water again and again after each time you apply some frosting to the cake. Apply a small amount at a time, and smooth as you go along. Keep your spatula slightly wet and it will be easier.

Toasted Coconut and Lime Biscotti

Max: This biscotti recipe is adapted from one I learned while working at a fishing lodge in Chilean Patagonia. The coconut and lime combination is not a traditional biscotti addition, but it will make a lively addition to coffee or next to some ice cream.

Desserts

 Dessert

 Makes about 24 biscotti

 Total time 45 minutes

1 cup unsweetened **dried coconut**

2 cups **all-purpose flour**

¾ cup **granulated sugar**

2 teaspoons **baking powder**

¼ teaspoon **salt**

¼ teaspoon **dried ginger**

zest of 1 **lime**

3 **eggs**

2 teaspoons **vanilla**

1   Preheat oven to 350° F.

2   Lightly toast coconut by laying on sheet pan and placing in oven for 5–10 minutes, until just barely beginning to brown. Remove from oven and set aside.

3   Mix well all ingredients except eggs and vanilla.

4   Add eggs and vanilla, and mix until mixture is completely moistened and no loose flour remains. The batter will be a little crumbly.

5   On a parchment-lined baking sheet, shape batter into two logs (you may have to smush them together), each about 3 inches wide, 12 inches long, and 1 inch high.

6   Bake for 30 minutes, until lightly brown. Remove from heat and let cool for 30 minutes on a wire cooling rack. Slice into ¼-inch slices and place back on parchment-lined baking sheet.

7   Bake slices again for 10–15 minutes, turning each slice over halfway through. Let cool until room temperature, if biscotti are not completely dried out and crispy, you can place them back in oven for 10–15 more minutes.

 Storage: Biscotti will keep for 1–2 weeks in an airtight container. If after that time, they start to get stale or soft, bake them again at 350°F for 10–15 minutes and they will last for another 1–2 weeks.

Crepes with Fresh Berries and Whipped Cream

These crepes are a surprisingly "light" dessert. Of course you can make these crepes for a Sunday brunch too. Feel free to experiment with the toppings—see below for some suggestions. While you can always buy ready to use whipped cream, try the homemade version at least once and you will be converted.

Desserts

 Dessert

 Serves 4

 Prep Time 15 minutes/Total time 30 minutes

Crepe Batter

1 cup **all-purpose flour**
2 tablespoons **sugar**
¼ teaspoon **salt**
3 eggs
5 tablespoons melted unsalted **butter**
1 ½ cups **milk**
1 teaspoon **vanilla**

Whipped Cream

1 pint **heavy whipping cream**
¼ cup **sugar**

Cooking and Assembly

1 quart fresh **strawberries**
vegetable oil for greasing pan
2 tablespoons melted **butter**
¼ cup **brown sugar**

Crepe Batter

1   In a large bowl or blender, mix together flour, sugar, and salt.

2   Add eggs and unsalted butter and mix thoroughly.

3   Add milk and vanilla extract in a steady stream, mixing constantly with a wire whisk or with the blender running until smooth and homogenous.

Whipped Cream

1   Beat the cream in a standing mixer, or using a hand mixer or wire whisk.

2   When cream thickens slightly, add sugar.

3   Continue beating until cream forms stiff peaks.

Cooking and Assembly

1   Remove the green tops from the strawberries, cut them into quarters and set them aside.

2   Heat a 10-inch nonstick skillet on medium heat and grease lightly with vegetable oil.

3   Pour ⅓-cup of batter into the skillet and lift the skillet so the batter reaches the edges.

4   Cook until lightly browned underneath, and the crepe puffs up slightly from air bubbles underneath, about 2–3 minutes. Flip with plastic spatula and cook for 1 more minute.

5   Cook all the crepes, you can stack them up on a plate and keep them warm in a barely heated oven.

6   To finish the crepe, mix the butter and brown sugar together, and spread some on a crepe. Sprinkle about a ¼-cup of strawberries in the middle, roll or fold up, then place a few more strawberries and a dollop of whipped cream on top.

Variations

Chocolate Peanut Butter Crepes: Melt 1-cup of semisweet chocolate chips with ½-cup of smooth peanut butter in a double boiler or in the microwave. Spread mixture on cooked crepes, fold or roll and serve.

Candied Ginger and Orange: Spread 2 tablespoons orange marmalade and 1 teaspoon candied ginger on each crepe.

Apple-Cinnamon: Peel, core, and slice 4 Granny Smith apples. Place in a medium saucepot with ¼-cup sugar, 2 tablespoons unsalted butter and 1-tablespoon cinnamon. Simmer until apples are tender and then spread on finished crepes.

Mint Chocolate Chip Cookies

Max: For a late night snack at my house in Ann Arbor, nothing can beat the chocolate chip cookie. At our house, many a night was spent baking some cookies and then watching a movie. We find ourselves continually pausing the movie to go grab more cookies because they are just that good. The mint adds an interesting twist on a classic flavor, but feel free to leave it out if it's not your thing.

Desserts

 Dessert

 Yields about 30 cookies

 Total time: 60 minutes

2 ¼ cups **all purpose flour**

1 teaspoon **baking soda**

1 teaspoon **salt**

1 cup (2 sticks) **unsalted butter**

¾ cup **granulated sugar**

¾ cup **brown sugar,** tightly packed

2 large **eggs**

2 teaspoons **vanilla extract**

½ teaspoon **mint extract**

2 cups **semisweet chocolate chips**

1 Preheat oven to 375°F.

2 Combine flour, baking soda and salt in a small bowl.

3 Beat butter, granulated sugar, brown sugar until creamy, light and fluffy.

4 Add eggs one a time, mixing in each egg before adding the next. Add vanilla and mint extract and flour mixture.

5 Mix in chocolate chips.

6 Place on cookie sheet, in rough balls about 2 inches across (cookies will melt and spread out during baking).

7 Bake for 10–11 minutes, depending on how you like them.

8 Cool on wire cooling rack.

 Tip: To keep cookies tasting fresh, place them (cooled to room temperature) in a zip-close plastic bag or airtight container.

brothers@freshmaninthekitchen.com

www.freshmaninthekitchen.com

Eli   Max

Max Sussman began his culinary education in a brief entrepreneurial attempt at selling homemade guacamole out of his parents' kitchen. Soon afterwards, he moved on to work at several Ann Arbor, Michigan restaurants. First was the Sunflower Café, a mostly vegetarian restaurant where he was initiated into the secrets of salad and pizza making. Later, he cooked for the masses as the Chef, alongside brother Eli, at Camp Tavor, a summer camp in Michigan. His classical training was honed at eve – the restaurant, whose chef was described by Mario Batali as having "unequivocally divine technique." To further his culinary experience Max is presently finishing up his tour as the Sous Chef at The Martin Pescador Lodge, a fly-fishing resort in Chilean Patagonia.

While pursuing his B.A. in American Culture in a leisurely style at the University of Michigan, he hosted his own radio program on WBCN, directed an award-winning documentary entitled "Whatever You Destroy," and was an editor of the bi-monthly magazine "Critical Moment." When not cooking he DJ's as Max Blixx and reads science fiction.

Eli Sussman, the much more sarcastic but only slightly taller brother, cooked alongside his brother Max, as the assistant chef, providing for those 200 hungry Michigan summer campers at Camp Tavor. Throughout college he worked at a Greek American restaurant where he perfected his trademark "in the air" omelet flip. He now moonlights as a chef for two of LA's finest catering companies.

Eli graduated from The James Madison College of Political Science at Michigan State University. Currently living in Los Angeles Eli's day job is a creative strategist and media-buying consultant for The Gary Group, which specializes in innovative solutions for the music, film, fashion and gaming industries. On the weekends you can probably find him at the beach boogie boarding (which he is pretty sure is for ten year olds but doesn't care) and reading a fiction novel he secretly wished he had written. Besides messing around in the kitchen cooking for friends, Eli loves to endlessly debate the content of all music and movies.

We'd like to thank:

Our parents—thanks for the inspiration and for pushing us, letting us try new ideas and following any dream no matter how obscure or seemingly impossible. From both of you we draw creativity, calmness through chaos and the ability to be leaders among men.

Our grandparents, aunts, uncles and cousins—thanks for the non-stop support, suggestions, recipe ideas, critiques, and for being our taste testers.

Tavor—the staff, the kitchen and the campers—thanks for the constant inspiration and criticism. For being a constant peanut gallery and teaching us how to work under extreme heat and pressure. Our experiences there made us who we are, in and outside of the kitchen.

All of our friends from Hillel, Berkley, Ann Arbor and East Lansing—thanks for supporting us and this book. We wouldn't have the outlook on life we have if you weren't always there for us. We made this book for you.

Everyone who came to the 421 potlucks, brunches, and barbeques, for indulging me by happily consuming the things I cook.

526 Sunset House—I saw a call for help from the masses. Thanks for giving inspiration by not knowing how to cook, grocery shop or clean. It was an awesome year.

The Lou Ha's "who's hungry crew"—we got through those Sunday morning kitchen shifts together. It helped shape the tone and the contents of this cookbook more than you will ever know. And thanks for enough good times to fill a really huge yacht.

Kate—for your support, inspiration, and advice

Eve Aronoff, Sergio Dominguez, and everyone else at eve-the restaurant—for being my culinary education and most excellent co-workers.

Elana and Debra—your help at the start allowed us to bring this from idea to reality. Thanks for the structural and editorial help.

Shel—thanks for the remarkable photos. You are a perfectionist and for that we are extremely grateful.

Anna and Frans—for putting up with last minute work on this book, for the encouragement, for the alternative title suggestions, and of course, for all the publicity to the guests of the Martin Pescador Lodge.

Mike—your vision and expertise is evident in the visual strength of this book as an innovative and useful cooking and teaching tool. Your collaboration was invaluable.

Shira and Steve—the dream publisher and editor duo. Each meeting, conference call and photo shoot was increasingly more exciting. Our own enthusiasm and passion fed off your passion for the project. We are so proud of what we accomplished together. Thank you for believing in two brothers who had something to say and to cook.

Index